HELEN LEE ROBINSON, editor

Guide's Greatest
SABBATH STORIES

REVIEW AND HERALD® PUBLISHING ASSOCIATION
HAGERSTOWN, MD 21740

The authors assume full responsibility for the accuracy of all facts and
quotations as cited in this book.

All Scripture references are from the *Holy Bible, New International Version*.
Copyright © 1973, 1978, 1984, International Bible Society. Used by permission of Zondervan Bible Publishers.

This book was
Edited by Helen Lee Robinson
Cover designed by FreshCut
Cover art by Ralph Butler
Electronic makeup by Shirley M. Bolivar
Typeset: 13/16 Goudy

PRINTED IN U.S.A.

08   07   06   05   5   4   3   2

R&H Cataloging Service
Guide's greatest Sabbath stories,
     compiled and edited by Helen Lee Robinson.

     1. Sabbath—Stories.   I. Robinson, Helen Lee, 1976-   .

                    263.2

ISBN 0-8280-1814-6

Contents

Also by Helen Lee Robinson:
   Guide's Greatest Prayer Stories
   Guide's Greatest Miracle Stories
   Guide's Greatest Escape From Crime Stories
   Guide's Greatest Christmas Stories
   PowerGuide LogBook 2

To order, call 1-800-765-6955.

Visit us at www.reviewandherald.com for information on other Review and Herald® products.

A special thanks to the authors we were unable to locate. If anyone can provide knowledge of their current mailing address, please relay this information to Helen Lee Robinson, in care of the Review and Herald® Publishing Association.

Introduction

The Sabbath—the seventh day of the week—was set apart by God at the time of Creation. That's what makes the Sabbath so extra special. Each week God invites us to spend the day with Him and to "remember the Sabbath day by keeping it holy" (Exodus 20:8).

This book contains 24 stories about people and their experiences with the Sabbath. You will read about answered prayers, encounters with angels, personal choices in tough times, rewards of faithfulness, discovery of the Sabbath, and much, much more. The stories are from *Guide* magazine, a weekly Christian magazine for young people.

I hope you enjoy reading the stories in this book. And my prayer is that you too will discover the blessings of the Sabbath day.

—Helen Lee Robinson

"For in six days the Lord made the heavens and the earth, the sea, and all that is in them, but he rested on the seventh day. Therefore the Lord blessed the Sabbath day and made it holy" (Exodus 20:11).

1

The Mysterious Test

by Anees A. Haddad

Sir, I'm sorry, but I cannot come to school tomorrow. It is God's Sabbath day, and the only school I attend on Saturdays is Sabbath school. There we study the Bible and—."

"Change that crazy idea of yours, Nour!" snapped the principal. "Every day belongs to God. What would we do if Ahmed quit school on Friday and you didn't come on Saturday and John refused to show up on Sunday? If we allowed such things to happen, this school would have to take a permanent vacation!"

"But, sir, the Sabbath is different, because—"

With an angry look the principal interrupted him. "Goodbye, Nour. We'll see you tomorrow."

Nour left the principal's office determined to obey God. He knew it might result in his dismissal from the government school. And in that whole country of more than 20 million people, his church did not have a single school. *If I am dismissed,* he thought, *where will I go?* When he arrived at home he entered his room and asked God to help him stand firm to the principles he knew were right. As he got up from his knees his heart was light and there was a peaceful smile on his face. *I will be as brave as Daniel and as true as Joseph!* he thought.

The days passed and became weeks, and weeks became months. Nour was never seen in the government school on Saturdays. His friends ridiculed him, and his teachers made fun of him. But for some reason he was not dismissed from school.

Then one day two professors were talking to each other. "What a bright student Nour is!" one said.

"Yes, if only he did not keep Sabbath on Saturday!" sighed the other. "I'm afraid he's going to find it tough at the end of the year!"

"You mean the exams?"

"Yes, exactly! What will he do if one of the exams falls on Saturday?"

"Oh, I think he'll take it. He won't lose a whole school year just to keep his Sabbath!"

At home Nour's family noticed that he was praying much more frequently than usual. More than once he was seen on his knees during the night pleading for strength to be "as brave as Daniel and as true as Joseph."

It was not long before the students were reviewing

for the first examination. Nour was intelligent, and all the other students knew it. "Nour, will you help me with this algebra problem?" they begged. "Let's review physics together, Nour; I need your help!" Nour was always glad to help, even those who laughed at his "funny ideas"!

Monday was a big day! Groups gathered here and there to cram last-minute facts for the examination. The bell rang. Hearts beat faster. The representative from the Ministry of Education stepped out of his car and was taken into the principal's office. A whisper passed among the students, "He will sign our certificates if we pass. He has to see the test papers, too!"

It was an eventful day. Nour knew that he had done very well, and he offered a prayer of thanksgiving. The next few days were not much different from Monday. Excitement, exams, smiles, and tears!

But all through the week a notice on the bulletin board reminded Nour of an exam scheduled for Sabbath morning. He swallowed hard. *I'll be in Sabbath school,* he thought, *but God will help me out.*

That Friday night Nour spent much time with God. It was late when he went to bed, and it seemed like he had been sleeping for just a few minutes when the morning sun brightened his bedroom. Nour had been praying that something would happen to stop the examination from being held on Sabbath, and now with peace in his heart, off to Sabbath school he went.

It wasn't a regular meeting place, for the church was not allowed to hold services in that country. The members grouped off in private homes and held their meetings secretly. They wanted to sing, but they dared not lift their voices lest they were heard by the police. Imprisonment would surely follow.

In the home where Nour went to worship, those present prayed especially for him in his trial. No sooner had they said Amen than a knock came on the door. With fear and trembling the hostess peaked through the upper window, and all eyes questioned, "Is it a police officer?"

"It's a boy," said the hostess as she started downstairs. Then she shouted from below, "Nour, come down! He wants you."

"Now what?" said Nour as he descended the steps. "Oh, good morning, Ali. Come in!"

"No—no—I—I—can't— Come quickly! Come to school!" Ali panted.

"What's the matter?" Nour asked.

"You see—you—your name was read just—just before the examination. When the inspector did not hear you say 'Present,' he asked about you. The principal exchanged winks with the other teachers in the hall and called me. 'Go quickly and tell him to come right now,' he said. So, I ran to your house, but did not find you. Your neighbor told me you were here. I came running all the way. Hurry, Nour, don't be foolish! You will lose your whole school year." Running up the street, he called over his shoulder, "You still have enough time to complete the test." His voice died in the distance.

Turning around, Nour started to climb the stairs back to Sabbath school. He told the other members, and they prayed together, asking God to intervene so that Nour would not have to repeat his school year just because of the one examination that occurred on the Sabbath day.

On Monday morning Nour went to school much earlier than usual. What were the results of the previous week, especially the Sabbath incident? Furthermore, what were the results of the countless prayers that had been offered in his behalf?

The principal called Nour to his office and told him to be ready for an appointment at 9:00. It was to be in the main hall. Very few students were on the campus, but Nour noticed that all the teachers were there. Were they going to dismiss him? Maybe their presence had nothing to do with him!

A little before 9:00 Nour went to the main hall. Upon entering the big room he was shocked to see the representative of the Ministry of Education. What was he doing there? Next to him was the principal, and all around were the teachers! The place looked like a judgment hall. Nour was frightened. He was the only student present.

"Sit at that desk, will you?" the principal said. A

dozen eyes rested upon him. Some faces were frowning; others were smiling! With trembling legs the boy sank into the seat at the appointed desk. In front of him was a folder.

"Open the folder and proceed," the principal announced.

Slowly and cautiously Nour opened the folder. Inside he saw examination questions! Unbelievable! His heart skipped a beat! Blood rushed to his face! He bowed his head and closed his eyes.

"He's praying," whispered a teacher. "He's certainly a courageous boy—a faithful fellow!"

Time fairly flew as he wrote the answers easily. Then he handed in his papers. "Thank you, professors. You are all very kind," he said courteously.

Nour's grades revealed that he was the top student in his class. He was honest, he was faithful, and he was brave—as brave as Daniel and as true as Joseph.

Until this day his unique examination is a mystery. Was a special examination ever given in that country so a boy could keep the Sabbath? Has one been given since? Most unlikely. But prayer changes things. And faith can move mountains—move tests, professors, principals, and government officials!

Today Nour is a professor in an Adventist college in the Middle East helping to train young people "to stand for the right though the heavens fall."

2

Private Ford's Sabbath Pass

by Lawrence Maxwell

Bob was in the Army. It was Friday after-noon, and he had not made arrangements to get Sabbath off.

He had been in the Army several weeks already, and had gotten Sabbaths off before. But there had been other Adventists with him then, and it had been easy to go in a group to speak to the officers.

This time Bob was alone. He had been moved from the camp where he had been stationed and brought to a new camp. He was the only Adventist here. He would have to go to the officers by himself.

He knew what he had to do. In one of the build-ings was a large room with a counter down the mid-dle. He would have to go into that room, where many soldiers would be milling around. He would stand at the counter, and a loud-voiced corporal, his feet propped on a desk, would shout at him, "What do you want, private?" He would tell him he wanted to see the first sergeant. "What for?" the corporal would demand. And he would have to tell him, shouting just as loudly, so that everyone in the room would be able to hear that he was a Seventh-day Adventist and wanted a Sabbath pass. The men would laugh at him. He knew they would.

Bob didn't like to be ridiculed any more than anyone else does. Was it really necessary to get a pass? No one in the camp knew he was an Adventist. If he didn't keep this Sabbath, no one would know he had been unfaithful. He would be here for only a few days. Before next Sabbath he would be at another camp, where there would be other Adventists to keep the Sabbath with.

But Bob knew this reasoning was wrong. He gathered up his courage and walked to the office. He stepped into the room and walked halfway to the counter—and his courage left him. He couldn't talk to those men. He couldn't face the laughter. He turned and went back to the barracks.

Friday afternoon was running out. He must get the pass. Again he started for the office, but this time got only halfway to the building before turning back.

At the barracks he scolded himself. "This won't do. I shall go and get that pass." And having firmly decided, Bob walked back to the office and up to the counter and told the corporal he wanted to see the first sergeant. It wasn't nearly as hard as he had thought. No one laughed. The corporal told him to step into the sergeant's office.

"Private Robert Ford reporting," he said to the sergeant. "I am a Seventh-day Adventist and would like a pass for Saturday."

He braced himself for the sergeant's icy remarks. To his surprise, the sergeant lifted a paper from the table and said, "I was told an Adventist was coming and have already signed your pass. Here it is."

You could have knocked Bob over with a feather!

Later, when he told the story in Sabbath school, he said, "That experience convinced me that God is ready to give us all the help we need to live right. It's just up to us to make the proper decisions."

3

School Fees for Jean and Gillian

by Margaret D. Clarke

The lights were out and the house was dark, but it was not silent. In the main bedroom, Mother and Father were talking in whispers. They were discussing budgets and money matters in a worried sort of way, and they did not want the children to hear.

"But do we really have to take the children out of church school?" Mother asked.

"Well," replied Father, "there's milk and bread and groceries and clothes and bank payments and the dentist's bill and—" Father did some arithmetic. He added up all the bills and subtracted them from the money in his paycheck. There was nothing left over—nothing at all for school fees.

In the other room, Jean and Gillian were also talking in whispers. They guessed about the money troubles, and they realized that the only expense that could be removed was church school tuition.

"If we have to go to public school, I suppose we have to," Jean said. "But I doubt they'll have a teacher as nice as Miss Cuzon."

"And just imagine going to school without Alene," moaned Gillian. Then a few seconds later she added, "I don't believe God wants us to leave. Somehow we'll get the fees."

Silence fell, and sleep crept in. But even in their dreams the girls saw dollars and cents and bills and school fees.

Next day, as Father stood working at his bench, the owner of the furniture-making business where he worked came up to him. "The business is expanding, and I want you to be the foreman of the new section I am adding," the boss said. "You get on well with the men, and I know you're an honest Christian." Then he added the very welcome words, "Of course, you'll receive a raise in pay."

"So you see," Father told the girls when he arrived home, "God has provided the money for church school."

Friday came, and the boss called Father aside. "Look here, I'm terribly sorry about this, but there's a traveling salesman coming tonight with samples. As foreman, you should see them. I know your beliefs about the Sabbath, and I promise it won't happen again, but I made the arrangements with the salesman before you became foreman. It will be only this once. Only once won't hurt, will it?"

Only once. The phrase went through Father's mind. Only once. But it would hurt. He'd be letting down his standards.

"I'm sorry, sir," he said. "I just can't."

The following week, when Harry had the chance, he spoke to his boss. "If my religion is going to hurt your business in any way, I would rather not be foreman. I'll understand if you put someone else in my place."

"Very well," the boss replied. Father couldn't tell what he was thinking.

That night Father said to the girls, "It looks as though you won't be going to church school very much longer."

"God will keep us there somehow," Gillian confided to Jean.

Friday was payday, and Father found more money in his envelope than even foreman's wages. He decided that there must have been a mistake. Then a horrible thought struck him. *What if this is the way the boss is using to lay me off? Maybe this is a bonus to soften the blow.*

Father's shoulders slumped a little as he entered the boss's office. "You've given me too much money, sir."

"Yes, I know."

There was an awkward pause. Then the boss said,

"I no longer require your services as foreman."

This is it, thought Father. *I don't have a job now.*

"No," continued the boss, "what this business needs is a production manager, and you're it."

Production manager! Father was dazed. That meant there would be money for church school fees and some left over. He knew there was a text somewhere in the Bible that said God is able to do more than we ask or think, but at the moment, he couldn't get the words right.

"I knew God would let us stay in church school," announced Gillian triumphantly, as she looked up the text for her father in Ephesians 3:20, 21: "Now to him who is able to do immeasurably more than all we ask or imagine . . . to him be glory."

4

When Grandpa Argued With an Angel

by Ben-Ira

The man who argued with an angel was Mr. G. T. van Druten. His granddaughter Mary Anna Lees told me all about it. Here is her story.

Mr. van Druten, my grandpa, was farming at the time in South Africa. His family had come from Holland, and he was a very devout Christian, a member of the Dutch Reformed Church.

When his son William was about 20 months old, the little boy suddenly became seriously ill with what seemed to be an asthma attack. Grandma became alarmed. "We have to get him to a doctor as soon as possible, or we might lose him," she said.

Grandpa agreed. He asked the hired men to prepare the spring wagon at once with a team of eight mules. They would have to take food and bedding, and servants to care for the mules; so it was quite an expedition.

Grandpa wasn't sure where to take his little boy. It was about 125 miles to Kimberley and a little more than 125 miles to Bloemfontein. There were no closer towns. Kimberley was a mining camp at the time, and Bloemfontein was a more settled community. The baby was so ill that it might be too late whichever way they went.

The first part of the journey did not call for any decision, but soon they were approaching the fork in the road where one turn led to Bloemfontein and the other to Kimberley. Grandpa prayed that God would give him a sign so that he would make no mistake in his choice.

Soon after he had prayed, he saw a horseman on the road that led to Bloemfontein. The road passed through open fields, where Grandpa could see miles in every direction. He knew that that horseman had not been on the road before he had prayed, and he also knew he had not gotten onto the road by riding across the fields. Grandpa was convinced that this was God's answer to his prayer. He decided to follow the horseman and turned the team toward Bloemfontein.

They had not gone far when the horseman disappeared. Grandpa called to the servant who was driving and asked him if he had seen the horseman. He said he had. But now neither of them could see him, and there was no shelter where he might be hidden. With gratitude to God and renewed hope that

Heaven's blessings would protect the little one till they reached help, they continued the journey.

This happened on a Saturday evening. As midnight drew near, Grandpa stopped the wagon and started to make camp.

Grandma protested strongly. "What are you stopping for? The baby is so sick, any breath might be his last. Even if we went on at once, it might be too late."

"We can't go on," Grandpa said. "It is now the Sabbath. I have never desecrated the day before and will not do so now." (Grandpa believed that Sunday was the Sabbath and that he should keep it holy from midnight until midnight.)

Grandpa was soon asleep. As he slept, he had a dream. He saw the horseman who had guided him at the fork of the road ride into camp and ask him why he had stopped and camped.

"I am camping here to keep the Sabbath," Grandpa told him.

"Which day is the Sabbath?" the horseman asked.

Grandpa replied, "Sunday, the seventh day, of course."

"You are mistaken," said the horseman. "Yesterday was the seventh day and the Sabbath. If you have a calendar, I will show you."

So, in his dream, Grandpa went to the wagon where Grandma had a box with a calendar in it, and he got it out. It was just as the horseman said, but

Grandpa was not convinced. "This must be a bad calendar," he said. "I will get a good one, and then you will see I am right."

The horseman disappeared, and Grandpa awoke. But he had a very troubled mind. He awakened Grandma and asked her if she had a good calendar.

"The one you have is a good one," she said.

"No, it isn't, for it shows Saturday as the seventh day of the week."

Grandpa got out his Bible to see if that would help him, but it just made matters worse. By daybreak Grandpa felt lost and uncertain about everything. "Let's keep going," he said. So they continued their journey to Bloemfontein.

Grandpa took Grandma and baby William to the doctor and left them there. Then he went at once to see the Dutch Reformed minister. The minister told him that the original Sabbath was Saturday, but it had been changed to Sunday, though he did not know who had changed it or when.

On his way back to the doctor's office, Grandpa met a Jewish Rabbi. He asked him about the Sabbath, and was told that the Christian church was responsible for the change. So Grandpa went back to the minister. They studied all day and came to the conclusion that Saturday was the Bible Sabbath. Grandpa kept the next Sabbath, and continued to keep it ever afterward.

Grandpa had a little cottage in Kimberley, where the family sometimes went for vacations. Soon after William got better they went there for a few days. On Sabbath they walked to the diggings—large diamond mines at Kimberley—and sat on a big rock to watch all that was going on.

They noticed a tent, and sitting in the door of the tent was a man dressed in a clean white suit reading his Bible. It was so different from the activities in the diggings that Grandpa and Grandma were fascinated by it. Finally they went over to find out who the man was. It was in this way that they met William Hunt.

William Hunt was a miner. While prospecting in the United States, he had found the Sabbath truth. Now he was a faithful keeper of the Sabbath. Later he gave Grandpa the address of the headquarters of the Seventh-day Adventist Church, and so opened the way for the first Seventh-day Adventist foreign missionaries to come to South Africa.

Grandpa was baptized by our pioneer missionary, Elder Charles Boyd, and was one of the first members of the Beaconsfield Church of Seventh-day Adventists. He was a faithful member until the day he died.

5

Sabbath Courage at Gunpoint

by Enid Sparks

It was a quiet Sabbath morning in the late spring of 1957, and Manuel Saigado was walking toward the little church in the village of Yarvicoya, Bolivia. As the rays of the sun came over the low hills, the Lord seemed very near him, and he hummed a tune.

Then he began to recall some of the Bible verses in the Sabbath school lesson. Foremost in his thoughts was Psalm 50:15, "Call upon me in the day of trouble; I will deliver you."

Why should a text like that seem so important on a beautiful morning like this? he wondered. *Is there trouble in store for me today?*

He entered the mud-brick chapel and saw at a glance that every low bench was already full. Many women and children were sitting on the floor.

Suddenly the calm was shattered by the roar of a truck that stopped with screeching brakes right in front of the chapel. The chapel door swung open, and a gruff voice shouted, "Everyone outside."

The worshipers saw rifles slung over the shoulders of the intruders. They obediently filed out.

"Who speaks for this group?" the leader barked.

The people stood trembling, wondering what they should do. Though their eyes were open, they were silently praying for guidance and protection.

"Speak up!" the officer growled.

Manuel stepped forward.

"You are to come with us to Oruro for a political demonstration," the officer said. "We have gained great victories and today we celebrate. Order your men into this truck at once. Do you hear?"

There was only silence. Manuel looked the officer steadily in the eye and said, "We cannot go! Today is the Sabbath. We are holding a religious service, not a political meeting." No one stirred.

This made the officer doubly angry. He took the rifle from his shoulder, stepped backward one pace, and aimed at Manuel's head. "Change your mind!" he snarled. "Come with us, or die!"

Some of the children wept. Several of the women knelt in the grass to pray. The angry man's finger stroked the trigger nervously.

"Today is the Sabbath of the God of heaven,"

Manuel answered, and his voice didn't even shake. "If I am to die for keeping God's Sabbath, I am ready."

"You mean you're not afraid? This is your last chance!" the leader declared fiercely.

"No, I am not afraid," Manuel answered. And lifting his eyes toward heaven, he committed himself into God's hands.

Just what happened in the next few minutes no one has ever been able to explain. But several of the men with rifles began climbing quickly into the truck. Soon the roaring vehicle was rumbling down the road, and the brave leader was doing his frantic best to scramble on amid cursing and swearing.

The worshipers filed back into the chapel and held a praise service before returning to their homes. They thanked God that He had answered their call for help.

And Manuel reverently proclaimed, "The saving power of God in the day of trouble cannot be denied."

6

The Hammer That Wouldn't Work on Sabbath

by Lawrence Maxwell

There was a shoemaker who lived in Spain. Let's call him Señor Menon, for I do not know his real name, though the story certainly happened. Señor Menon was a poor shoemaker, so poor that he owned only one hammer. He also had a radio that kept him company while he worked.

One day over this radio came the sound of a quartet singing "Lift up the trumpet and loud let it ring." Then a man talked about the love of God and some of the other important doctrines of the Bible.

"Good sermon; good singing," Señor Menon muttered to himself. "I must tune in again next week." He listened to the program many more times. And the more he heard, the more he liked it.

Then one morning a man selling books entered

his shop. "How interesting!" Señor Menon exclaimed as he examined the salesman's books. "These books say the same things I hear on the radio every week."

"You mean on the Voice of Prophecy program?" the book salesman asked.

"The very one," the shoemaker replied. "I know just about everything the Adventists teach by now."

"I'd be glad to come around and answer any questions you may have," the book salesman said. And so every evening for a week or two the colporteur visited the shoemaker and studied the Bible with him.

Señor Menon accepted everything except just one point. "The seventh-day Sabbath," he said, shaking his head. "There is no use telling me God wants us not to work on Saturday."

"But, Señor Menon," the colporteur said, "it says right here in your own Bible: 'The seventh day is a Sabbath to the Lord your God. On it you shall not do any work' (Exodus 20:10). Isn't that clear?"

"No, no." Señor Menon shook his head again. "You read the words clearly enough, but they do not mean what you say they mean."

"Señor Menon," the colporteur said, "if God were to send you a sign telling you He wants you to keep Saturday holy, would you keep it then?"

"Oh, yes, yes," Señor Menon said, "of course. I want to obey God."

The very next Sabbath Señor Menon went to

work as usual. But he couldn't find his hammer. Search high and low, in the cupboards and under the workbench, there was no hammer. And since that was the only hammer he had, he couldn't work that day.

He went back Sunday morning—and there was the hammer as large as life!

"A strange thing," he whispered. "Is this the Lord's sign? But no, it couldn't be. What's so important about losing a hammer for a day?"

So he went to work the next Sabbath too. He had no trouble finding the hammer this time. He carefully adjusted a shoe, slipped a nail from between his teeth, and put it exactly where he wanted it in the shoe. Then he struck the nail with the hammer. But as the hammer came down, its iron head broke into two pieces.

"It is the sign of the Lord!" the shoemaker cried. "My hammer wouldn't work last Sabbath, and it won't work today. And if it won't work on Sabbath, I won't either. From now on I shall keep the Sabbath." As soon as possible after that he was baptized. When the ceremony was over, the pastor handed him a gift.

"Here is a new hammer for you," the minister said. "I am sure it will never work on God's Sabbath."

"It won't," Señor Menon promised.

And it never has.

7

Phoning for Truth

by Barbara Westphal

anuel had hardly entered his teens when he left his home in Central America and began to earn his own living. First he worked as a messenger boy and later as a telegraph operator.

One day he approached his boss and said to him, "I'd like to go to a dance. Will you excuse me from work early so that I can go?"

"I'll give you permission, but on one condition," the boss said.

"And what is that, señor?"

"Promise me not to drink. If you get drunk and miss work one more day, you will be fired." It wasn't the first time Manuel's employer had reproached him for getting drunk and missing work.

Manuel didn't want to lose his job, so he

quickly promised, "Oh, thank you. I'll just dance. I won't drink."

But Manuel's promise was forgotten as soon as he was with his friends and glasses were passed around. The next day Manuel didn't go to work, nor the day after that. He was too sick. Besides, he was ashamed to face his boss, and he knew he would be dismissed.

On the afternoon of the second day his employer came looking for him. He said in a mocking tone, "Well, you really had a good time at that party, didn't you? What fun!"

"I didn't mean to take a drink." The boy groaned miserably, not daring to look the man in the eye. "Somehow I couldn't say no. And now you are through with me and I've lost my job."

"No," answered the employer kindly, "I'm not through with you. If I dismissed you now, you wouldn't be able to get another job. But you've got to stop drinking. You're going to be nothing but a tramp, a hobo, the way you are going now. You'll never amount to anything."

"I'll change!" sobbed the boy. "You've been so kind to me, and I won't disappoint you. With God's help I'll never take another drink in my life."

"You'll need help all right, and you might get help from reading the Bible."

"The Bible? Where could I get one?"

"I have one I can lend you."

"Oh, no, thank you. I couldn't read yours, for it would be a Protestant Bible. I would have to read a Catholic Bible, because I am a Catholic."

So Manuel went to his priest and borrowed a Catholic Bible. He had no idea where to begin or how to find the different Bible books, but day after day he took time to read instead of drinking.

One day he saw a well-dressed gentleman reading a Bible, and he decided to talk to him. "Is that a Bible you are reading?" he asked by way of introduction.

"Yes, it is. Do you like to read the Bible too?"

"Yes, I do. But I read the Catholic Bible. Yours looks different. Is it a Protestant Bible?"

"Yes, it is, but you will discover that they are very much alike. Why don't you come to our church? We study the Bible a great deal, and I'm sure you would enjoy our services."

Manuel thanked the man, who turned out to be a minister, and said he would visit their church. If he liked what they were teaching, he would become a member.

But when he attended the man's church, Manuel was disappointed. He didn't sense God's Spirit there. Besides, as he read his Bible every day, he was learning things that puzzled him. The seventh day was evidently the Sabbath day, and yet this church and all the others he knew of said the first day was the Sabbath. He stopped attending.

When the minister met him on the street one day, he asked Manuel why he had stopped coming to church.

"Oh, I'm studying the Bible at home," Manuel said.

"But you said you would become a member of our church."

"Yes, but I don't think that your church teaches the truth as the Bible presents it."

"Why, what do you mean, boy?"

"The Bible says that the seventh day is the Sabbath, but you have services on Sunday."

"Oh, you must be one of those *sabatistas!*" the minister exclaimed in disgust.

"*Sabatistas!* You mean there is a church that keeps the seventh day? Who are they? Where do they have their meetings?"

"I don't know," was all the minister would say.

Manuel began to ask his friends where the sabatistas held their meetings, but no one seemed to know. They had never even heard of such a church.

Time went on. Then one day when Manuel was working in the telegraph office he had a bright idea. He would look up the list of all the churches in the telephone directory and find the one called "*sabatista.*" But he looked in vain. There was no church called *sabatista,* or anything like it. So Manuel decided to phone each church and ask whether they kept the Sabbath day.

Ring-a-ling-ling. "*Hola*. Does your church keep Saturday or Sunday?"

"Sunday, of course, and we'll be glad to—"

"Thank you," said Manuel, and politely hung up.

Ring-a-ling-ling. "*Hola*. Does your church keep Saturday or Sunday?"

"Sunday, of course, and—"

"Thank you."

So Manuel went down the list. It was discouraging. All the churches answered him as if he were crazy. Of course, they all said, *of course* they had their services on Sunday!

There was one more church to call, and that was listed as the Mission Adventista, whatever that meant.

Ring-a-ling-ling. "Does your church keep Saturday or Sunday?"

"We keep the Sabbath, the seventh day of the week," a pleasant voice answered him.

"Really! When do you have your services?"

"At 9:00 on Saturday morning, and you are welcome to attend."

At 9:00 the next Sabbath morning Manuel was looking for the Mission Adventista. There was the big building, with a school beside it, right on Avenida Norte. The minister was friendly, and so were all the young people.

Manuel attended every meeting he could, but his boss was most unwilling to let him off work on

Saturdays. The man who had been so patient with Manuel when he was a good-for-nothing drunk had no patience at all with this religion, even though it was making him trustworthy and honest.

"I am going to stop work at the end of the month, señor," Manuel announced one day.

"Boy, you're crazy! I don't want to lose you. What's the matter?"

"I want to attend church on Saturdays, and you are never willing to let me have the day off, so I'd better stop working here."

"Think it over, son. Don't give up a good job. You don't have any relatives you can go to. What will become of you? There are thousands of unemployed people here in San Salvador, and you'll never find another job."

But Manuel was determined.

"I'm glad you've made your decision," the minister said kindly when he heard about what had happened. "And now what are you going to do to earn a living?"

"I don't know. I have no plans at all," Manuel replied. "God will have to help me."

The minister suggested that Manuel could become a literature evangelist. "You could sell books and earn money to go to school. You really should get more education."

With relief in his voice, Manuel thanked him, but

told him that it was rather late for him to try to go to school. Here he was a grown young man, and he had been to school only two years. It would be years before he could train for a profession.

But the beginning of the next school year found Manuel attending the little elementary school beside the church, sitting at the desks with boys and girls 10 years younger than he. He passed the eighth grade at the end of the year and took the government examinations.

He is working hard selling books, determined to secure a Christian education and serve God as a minister or a teacher.

8

Courage After Five Years

by Barbara Westphal

George Putten wished he didn't have to work on Saturdays, now that he had learned that the seventh day was the Sabbath. He worked for a large oil company in Aruba, and every time he asked his boss for Sabbaths off, his boss said no.

Five years went by, and Mr. Putten was unhappy every Sabbath because he wanted to be at Sabbath school. But he didn't want to lose his job because he had a wife and children to take care of.

One day he went to the missionary and asked him what he should do. Elder Hamm told him to ask his boss again if he could have his Sabbaths free, and if his request was refused, to stay away from work on Sabbath and go back on Monday.

"Don't quit your job," the missionary told him. "Keep going back. The company can't fire you in less than three weeks." According to the laws of Aruba a man cannot be fired without being given three notices, and the notices must be a week apart.

Mr. Putten did as he had been advised. He asked to have Saturdays off, but the foreman refused, so Mr. Putten stayed away from work that Sabbath. When he went to work Monday morning, his time card was not in the rack with the others. He asked the boss where it was, and the boss said, "You quit the job."

"Oh, no, I haven't. I'm not quitting a good job I've had for 12 years."

"Well, there will be no work for you to do until Wednesday."

That meant that Mr. Putten worked only on Wednesday, Thursday, and Friday that week. He got no pay for Monday and Tuesday, the days he didn't work. On Sabbath he was at Sabbath school once again.

On Monday morning when he went back to work, again his time card was missing. This time the foreman said, "There will be no work for you until Thursday." So that week Mr. Putten worked only on Thursday and Friday. That week he attended Sabbath school for the third time.

On Monday he went to the big boss, the manager, and told him about his problem. "I would like to help you," the manager said, "but we don't have a job for a man who cannot work on Saturdays."

Mr. Putten said, "I know one job you have where I could have the Sabbath free."

"What's that?"

"The cleaning squad."

"Oh, yes, but you wouldn't want to work sweeping and scrubbing for only nine guilders a day after you have been earning 14 guilders at a good job." (A guilder is a Dutch coin.)

Mr. Putten knew that if he earned only nine guilders a day, there would be barely enough money for food, and nothing for clothes for his children. But he said to the manager, "I would be willing to work for nine guilders if I could keep God's Sabbath."

"Then you must be crazy, and we have no jobs for crazy men! Do you have a family?"

"Oh, yes."

Then the big boss got really angry and told Mr. Putten to leave his office at once. "You are absolutely crazy," he shouted.

But as Mr. Putten was walking sadly down the hall, the manager called him back. "I'm not sorry for your wife, because she must be crazy too or she would not have married you. But I do feel sorry for your little children. You can work on the cleaning squad for nine guilders a day and have your Sabbaths free if you want to."

Can you guess what happened after that? Mr. Putten worked only one day on the cleaning squad.

After that the manager told the foreman to let him have his old job back with Sabbaths off. The next day the foreman came around and called Mr. Putten back to work in the shop.

And the manager told Mr. Putten, "I am going to pay you 14 guilders for the day you worked on the cleaning squad, and your full pay, too, for those Mondays and Tuesdays and that Wednesday when we told you there wasn't any work for you to do."

So, you see, when Mr. Putten finally got up enough courage—after five years—to be really firm about keeping the Sabbath, God helped him.

9

The Broken Radio

by Corrine Kandoll Vanderwerff

Judy walked out of the cafeteria and hurried across the campus to the dormitory. She had just enough time to get changed before Sabbath school began.

"Hey, sleepyhead," she chided when she found her roommate still in bed. "That's no place to be at this time on a Sabbath morning."

Doris turned her head to look at Judy. "Sleepyhead, nothing," she croaked.

"What happened to you?" Then without waiting for an answer, Judy said, "I'll put your name on the nurse's list on my way to church, OK?"

Doris nodded. "Some bug got me during the night. I sure wish I didn't have to miss Sabbath school and church."

"There's always the radio," Judy said. "That's one

nice thing about this place. You can listen to Sabbath services in your room."

"What radio?"

"Oh, that's right. Mine quit working last week. I'll run down to Irene's room and see if she's still around. I'm sure she'd let you use hers."

Without waiting for a reply Judy left the room. She knocked on Irene's door, but there was no answer. The door was locked. Evidently Irene was gone. Most of the other girls would be in Sabbath school by now too.

Judy felt sorry for her roommate. She returned to the room, wondering how she could help. "Everyone's gone," she said. "I wish I could help you."

"Let's try your radio," Doris suggested.

"Well, I could get it out. I was going to take it over to the shop yesterday to have it repaired, but never got around to it."

Judy went to the closet, thinking that it was hopeless. But she wanted to cheer Doris, so she decided to try to make it work. She took out the radio and set it on the table. Then she plugged it in and set the dial. There was a crackling, and then organ music filtered out of the speaker.

"It works!" Judy exclaimed. "But it was as dead as anything last Wednesday when I tried to use it."

Doris smiled. "I thought it would work."

"Well, I'd better hurry and get to church or I'll

never find a place to sit. I won't forget to put your name on sick list. Enjoy the services."

"I'll be here when you get back," Doris assured her.

When church service was over, Judy hurried back to the dormitory. "Well, how'd you enjoy the sermon today from the comfort of your pillow?" she teased as she walked in.

"It was lovely," Doris replied. "Do you know that until today I've never missed a single church service since I was a little girl. I'm so glad your radio worked. Even if I wasn't in church, I at least heard church. When you went to see if Irene was in her room this morning, I said a little prayer that if you couldn't find someone to borrow a radio from, your radio would work just for this morning."

Judy was impressed. "I knew that radio couldn't work by itself."

Later that evening Judy decided to test her radio. She turned it on. There was not a sound. She turned the dial and twisted all the knobs. She thumped the case. She did everything she could think of to make the radio play. Still it would not make a sound. And it never did work again until she took it to the repair shop and got it fixed.

10

The Mysterious Porter

by Edna Jewell

I need 10 porters to carry my loads. Go find them," commanded the chief.

Kapito hastened to do his bidding. Over the hills he walked, informing one man after another that the chief would need him the next day. At last he came to Elia's house. He knew the boy would make a good carrier, for he was strong and honest.

"Be sure to be on hand at dawn," he told Elia.

"But, Kapito," Elia said, "you know that I am a Seventh-day Adventist. I do not like to start a long trip on Friday."

"Yes, I know," Kapito said. "But the chief needs you this time. Besides, you'll probably arrive at your destination before your rest day begins, so why worry?"

Early the next morning the porters lined up in front of the chief's house. Each man was given a pack.

"You must be at Mzimba before sundown today," the chief commanded. "Now go."

The chief was transported without any discomfort to himself. A chair was slung between two poles, and four extra porters carried him.

Elia was happy when he heard that they were to be at the end of their journey before Sabbath. As he walked along with the rest of the men he made his plans. He would receive his pay, buy some food for the Sabbath, perhaps find an Adventist school nearby, and visit with fellow Christians. Then he would return home on Sunday.

But Elia's plans didn't work out the way he expected. Elia did reach Mzimba long before the sun set. But the chief was not traveling with the regular porters, and it was long after dark before he arrived at camp.

After eating the cold potatoes he had brought from home, Elia rolled up in his blanket and lay down under the stars—but not before he had asked his heavenly Father to watch over him during the night.

Long before any of the men thought of stirring, Kapito came to arouse them.

Elia sat up. "But I thought this was the end of our journey. Do we have to go farther? But—but—this is my Sabbath. I cannot carry a load today."

"You will have to tell the chief," answered Kapito. "I'll go with you."

"Wait a minute." Elia stood up and walked behind some bushes. He dropped to his knees. "God, You are my refuge and strength," he prayed. "Please be with me now."

Together the two walked to the chief.

At first the chief tried to bribe Elia, offering him gifts if he would carry his load. But Elia said he had to obey God first. The chief was infuriated and called for his whip. Two men threw Elia to the ground. They pulled off his clothes and left him lying on his face with only a loincloth around his waist.

The hippo-hide whip sang through the air and crashed with a dull thud on the bare back. A second time the whip screamed down on the lad. After the fifth lash, blood began to flow.

"Now are you going to obey me?" shouted the angry chief.

Elia spoke faintly, but there was no wavering. "If you will just give me a chance, I will carry your load after the sun sets. You will have it before you are up tomorrow."

"Very good, we'll see, but you will carry a double load, 88 pounds instead of 44."

The chief ordered the porters to tie two bundles together and leave them with the "seven-days" man, and no one was to give him food. Without a word the porters did as they were ordered, and Elia was left alone.

Elia shivered and slowly bent down to pick up his

clothes. His back was still bleeding. He knew that soon the flies would be attracted to the wounds. He carried the heavy load to an umbrella tree not far away, so that when the sun came up he could rest in its shade.

Then he knelt down and prayed, "Help me today to keep my thoughts on things of heaven so that I will not notice my hunger or my pain." Although he didn't have a Bible with him, he repeated Bible verses he had memorized. That Sabbath he felt Jesus very near to him as he sat alone under the tree.

As the setting sun painted magic colors in the sky, Elia knelt once more to ask for protection on his journey. Then he stood up very carefully. Every movement was agony. Scabs had formed on the open welts, and as he stretched, the wounds cracked open. He could feel the slow, warm trickle of blood down his back. How could he possibly walk all those miles with that heavy load?

In the distance he heard the terrifying cry of a hyena. Elia stumbled forward, but gradually his steps slackened as he grew more thirsty. And he was faint from hunger.

He was just going to sit down when he thought he heard the sound of water. Off to the side, through the bushes, yes, there it was. He began to drink deeply.

"Thank You, Jesus. That was wonderful," he whispered as he returned to take up his load.

"Would you like some freshly baked potatoes?"

Elia turned in surprise. There stood a man with a white cloth bundle in his hand. "My Master said I was to bring these to you. Eat them. You will find them very good."

Never had Elia tasted such delicious sweet potatoes.

"That was wonderful," he said as he stood up once more. All the stiffness seemed to have left his back. When he turned to lift his load, he saw that his new friend had placed it on his own head.

Elia was puzzled. Was this man another porter? He had never met him on any of his other journeys. But he set off with him along the path. As they walked and talked, heaven seemed to come down to earth for Elia. On and on they walked.

The first gray streaks of dawn were tinting the sky when the mysterious porter stopped. "I have to be going now. Do you think you can carry the load?"

Elia apologized for having let him carry it so far.

Carefully the stranger placed the bundles in position on Elia's head. The back string, which held them together, slipped a little, and the stranger stepped behind Elia to tie them more securely.

"It is firm once more," he said. "Goodbye and God bless you."

Elia turned to thank him—but he was alone. Though the valley was open for miles around, there was no trace of anyone.

"He was an angel!" Elia exclaimed. "Oh, I am the luckiest man on earth! I have walked with an angel!" With renewed energy, Elia sped over the ground.

Kapito and the porters were still rolled up in their blankets when Elia picked his way around them to the grass shack where the chief slept.

"*Odi, odi,*" he called. "Good morning, Chief."

The chief's mouth dropped open. "You have done the impossible! You should have fallen by the way. I expected to send men back for you, and then I would have been able to punish you again."

Elia answered slowly. "I don't doubt that you thought it was impossible for me to come with my injured back and the double load, but God promised to be my refuge and strength, and He has kept His word."

11

Sabbath in Jail

by Elfriede Volk

Frank Schwarz did not think of himself as a criminal, yet here he was, in the courthouse, with a case coming up against him. It seemed so strange, so unreal. But the hard wooden bench he was sitting on was real—as real as the 1921 calendar on the wall and the flag beside the judge's bench—the flag of one of the great nations of Europe.

The bailiff's voice droned through the courtroom as the officer read charges of petty theft against a small, grungy-looking man. The case did not interest Mr. Schwarz, so he looked around at the other offenders. There was a middle-aged man with a ruddy face who was obviously still under the effects of too much alcohol. Beside him sat two teenagers smiling self-consciously. Next to them was a flippant young woman. Beside her was a shifty-eyed little man with baggy pants and an oversize jacket. Mr. Schwarz himself was next. At the very end of the row sat a man in dirty rags.

The gavel rapped, arousing Mr. Schwarz from his reverie. "Next case," called the judge.

The bailiff called forward the man with the dirty rags, and Mr. Schwarz went back to studying the people on the bench beside him. *What are they accused of?* he wondered. *Are they criminals, or just victims of misunderstanding and misfortune?*

The judge's gavel rapped again, and the bailiff called, "Frank Schwarz."

As Mr. Schwarz walked to the front he felt all eyes fixed on him.

"You are charged with an offense under the education act. On four separate occasions you have refused to let your children attend school on Saturday. How do you plead, guilty or not guilty?"

Mr. Schwarz's throat felt very dry. "Guilty," he managed to say.

"You know the penalty for such an offense?" asked the judge.

"Yes, Your Honor."

"Then why did you do it?"

Mr. Schwarz took a deep breath. This was what he had been waiting for, even hoping for—a chance to explain. He knew that attendance at school was compulsory six days a week, yet he could not bring himself to break God's commandments in order to obey the law of the land. He prayed for divine help as he was about to present his case.

"Your Honor," he began, "I am a Seventh-day Adventist, and believe in the seventh-day Sabbath, which God says to keep holy. This Sabbath is Saturday. The commandment also applies for my children—"

"Seventh-day Adventist?" interrupted the judge. "Never heard of them. Anyway, there is nothing in the books about them. But you seem like a reasonable fellow, so if you will forget your notions and let your children attend school on Saturdays, I can dismiss the charge against you."

"Thank you, Your Honor," replied Mr. Schwarz, "but I cannot do that. I believe Saturday is God's Sabbath, and it would be a sin for me to send my children to school on that day."

"Very well then," said the judge, angered by Mr. Schwarz's apparent stubbornness, "you can take the consequences of your refusal. Fifty marks or three days in jail. You can pay the clerk."

All that week Mr. Schwarz debated what to do. Should he pay the fine? That would be much more pleasant than spending time in a musty cell. But could he afford to pay? If he continued to refuse to send the children to school on the Sabbath, he would have to pay 50 marks each month. But when would he find time to spend in jail? He could not afford to take time off work to put in his three days. Three whole days would be 72 hours.

When Friday morning came, he slipped his Bible into his lunch box and packed a set of clean clothes. He felt very strange when he said goodbye to his family that morning and walked out to work with his clean clothes under his arm.

As soon as the closing whistle blew he hurried up the mine shaft and into the shower room. As he was scrubbing off the coal dust he thought of home. His wife would be adding last-minute touches to the Sabbath meal, which she always prepared on Friday afternoon. Their oldest son would be sitting on the front steps, giving an extra shine to the family's shoes. And their daughter would be setting the table in preparation for the evening meal. The food was always ready on the table when he came home on Fridays. But today there would be one less place to set, for he was not going home.

Quickly Mr. Schwarz stepped out of the shower and dried himself. Soon he was dressed in his clean suit. Tucking his Bible under his arm, he walked out through the gate and headed directly for the city jail.

"Well, you're a good one!" exclaimed the warden in surprise. "Usually we have to drag people here by force, yet here you walk in of your own free will." Still shaking his head, he led Mr. Schwarz to a cell.

That Sabbath was the first of many Mr. Schwarz

spent reading his Bible in the city jail. He remained true to his convictions, so once a month, as soon as work was over on Friday, he walked directly to the city jail. The warden came to expect him, and never bothered to lock him in. On Monday morning his wife brought him his lunch so that he could go directly to work again. He had not yet spent the full 72 hours in jail, so every six or seven weeks he spent an extra Sabbath in the cell.

Eventually the law was changed so that the children of Jews and Seventh-day Adventists were exempt from attending school on Saturdays. But before that time came, Mr. Schwarz spent many Sabbaths in jail.

I wonder: If we had a law forcing us to attend school on the Sabbath, what would we do? Would we stand true to principle during difficult times? Then why not now?

12

Before the Rain Came

by Myrle Tabler

As Terry ran downstairs with his books under his arm, he heard voices in the kitchen. One was loud and argumentative, the other quiet.

"The boys will have to cut and shock the corn this weekend. A rain will ruin it." That was Grandpa Mynter, and he sounded determined.

Cut corn on Sabbath? thought Terry. He could not hear his mother's reply.

Just then Arden, halfway out the front door, called back, "Hurry, Terry, we'll miss the bus!"

Terry dashed after his brother. The school bus, full of laughing, chattering boys and girls drew up to the curb, and the boys jumped on. Arden joined in the fun, but Terry was quiet, wondering what to do.

"Look after things while I'm gone," his father had

told him, and Terry had felt proud and grown-up. He liked to please his dad.

Terry was 14, and Arden was 12. Their father worked in the nearby city during the week and drove home Saturday afternoons. The boys took care of the family cow and did chores before and after school. But to cut and shock a small field of corn for winter feed for the cow would take almost two full days.

Should he obey Grandpa, who owned the land, or should he obey God who had commanded that the Sabbath day be kept holy? Whatever he did, Arden would probably follow his example.

Mother was a Seventh-day Adventist, but Father was not. To him his wife's religion was "foolishness." Terry felt sure that his dad would agree with Grandpa Mynter.

There was no Seventh-day Adventist church nearby for Mother and the boys to attend, so they conducted their own weekly Sabbath school at home. Some of their friends liked to drop in on Sabbath mornings to hear Bible stories and sing hymns. They knew they were always welcome. But what would they think if they found the boys working in the field on Sabbath?

During recess Terry joined in the ball game, but his heart was not in it. After making several fumbling plays, he abandoned the game and sat down on the grass to watch. In a few minutes Arden joined him.

"What's the matter, Terry? Don't you feel good?"

Terry explained.

"Well, today is only Tuesday. Maybe something will happen before Sabbath." Arden tried to sound cheerful.

Terry sat up straight. "I just thought of something I saw on the bulletin board. There's a teachers' meeting next week, so we'll have two days of vacation. We can do the corn then."

Arden was not so sure. "Do you think Grandpa and Dad will let it wait till then?"

The boys did not have long to wonder. Grandpa Mynter was waiting for them when they arrived home after school.

"Now remember, you boys are to shock corn Saturday."

Arden explained that they could do it the following week because of a teachers' meeting.

"That corn won't wait another week! The kernels are beginning to shell out. It's time you got over this 'Sabbath' fanaticism!" He turned angrily away, pausing for a parting threat. "I'll talk to your father about this!"

"Whew!" said Arden. "He'll make trouble for us when Dad gets home. It'll be hard on Mother too. What'll we do?"

Terry had no answer.

Mother and the boys prayed about the problem that evening at worship. Mother reminded them,

" 'God is our refuge and strength, an ever present help in trouble' " (Psalm 46:1).

But Terry was not sure. He lay awake long after his brother was asleep. Finally he got up and knelt by his bed. "Dear Jesus," he prayed, "help me to do what is right no matter what happens—even if the corn spoils and Dad and Grandpa punish us."

He could sleep now, for he had made up his mind.

"You don't seem worried today," Arden said as they dressed for school.

"No, I feel as if everything will be all right."

But sure as he was, even Terry was not prepared for the principal's announcement in assembly that Wednesday morning. He could hardly believe what he heard.

"Something unexpected has come up," the principal announced. "Our chief speaker will not be able to come next week, but he can come this week, so we have moved teachers' meeting to this Thursday and Friday. There will be no school on these days."

The boys' father drove home Saturday afternoon just as the rain was beginning to fall. As he passed the corn patch, he looked out the window and saw shocks standing tall and safe in the cut-over field.

Thanks to the mysterious change in the teachers' meeting, Terry and Arden had been able to obey their father and keep the Sabbath too.

13

Freedom Letter

by Siegfried Grentz

Trying to hide her troubled face, 13-year-old Emma hurried about the crowded immigrant barracks helping Mother care for the other children. She pulled her younger brother Eddy into a chair and started to comb his unruly black hair.

"If you don't sit still, you won't have any hair left," she said, bringing the comb down on his head with a snap.

What is wrong with me today? she wondered. *Why am I so angry? I was never this way when we were at home.*

Her family would never have left their lovely Romanian home if it had not been for the German leader Adolf Hitler. Hitler was determined to bring the "super race" back home and lead them on to conquer the rest of the world. He had Germans from all points of the compass returning back to the fatherland.

Emma's family, who had been traveling with four other Seventh-day Adventist farming families, were under quarantine for six weeks in this reentry camp. Camp rules dictated that everyone help with the work.

On the first Saturday they refused to work because it was their Sabbath. The camp leader screamed at them, "A repeat performance of this violation will not be tolerated!"

The next Sabbath found the Adventists studying their Bibles, singing hymns, and thanking God for His care and protection. The camp leader was about to discipline the families when he received a notice that a Nazi officer would inspect the camp the following Sabbath. A cruel smile passed over the camp director's face. Yes, the visiting inspector would most certainly deal with the problem.

The sudden rattle of a rusty door lock brought Emma back to camp life with a start. Father appeared in the doorway. "Hurry the children, Mother!" he called as he finished buttoning the freshly washed shirt he wore on Sabbaths. "The entire camp must be at the main hall in five minutes!" Trouble hung over his face like a tattered veil.

Deathly silence pervaded the gray limestone building where the sudden metallic heel clicks of two guards announced the arrival of the Nazi officer. In the vast crowd the group of Adventists waited near one end of a well-washed table. They stood as still as statues while the Nazi officer came to a halt in the middle of the freshly waxed floor.

"Well," he snapped, "the Third Reich doesn't have all day. What's the problem here?"

A heavyset man shuffled from the crowd and identified himself as the camp leader. "You see, sir," he said, pointing a finger at the Adventists, "these Jews don't want to work on their holy day."

The mention of Jews and their refusal to work made the officer's face take on the hard coldness of a windswept iceberg. His eyes scanned the accused group.

The spokesperson for the Adventist families replied, "Sir, our religious convictions do not allow us to work on Saturday, which is our Sabbath. Also, we are not Jews but German—"

"Do you think the Führer [Hitler's title] has time to sit around and worry about your God's Sabbath?" the Nazi snapped back.

"*Nein, nein, Herr Offizier*, but we would be glad to work on Sun—"

"I've heard enough," the officer barked, bringing his fist down on the table in a resounding crash. With the force of an erupting volcano the Nazi hurled threats at his victims. He continually punctuated each sentence with a crashing fist, which caused the neatly stacked plates on the far end to tremble. In conclusion he stated, "I will give you people exactly five minutes to decide whether or not you will work on Saturday."

Within five seconds came their determined but respectful reply. "We cannot and will not work on the Sabbath, though the heavens fall!"

"What?" screamed the astonished Nazi, almost dropping his pince-nez eyeglasses. "Well, then," he stammered, "I hope your God can hear through the walls of a concentration camp!" And with that he spun on his heel and stalked out of the building. Camp inmates were released to resume their day's work.

But the talk of the camp was centered on the Adventists. What was going to happen to them? Would they really be sent to a concentration camp? Would God honor their faith and sincerity?

Within a week the camp leader, who had been the first official to threaten the Adventist families, was discovered to have been stealing food from the kitchen. He was dismissed.

As he was leaving, Emma's father helped him load his luggage onto the train. "Listen to me," the man said to Emma's father. "Forget this religious business. These Nazis aren't kidding. They will kill all of you." With that he boarded the train.

A new camp director moved into the office. He was troubled about one thing: What should he do about the Adventists? He called the Adventist immigrants before him and spoke to them. "I can sympathize with you, because I am also a Christian. But I am still an army officer. I must obey orders. But there is one thing I can do to help you. I will send a letter of appeal to the only man under Hitler who can save you from the concentration camp. That man is Heinrich Himmler, head of the German Secret Police."

About three weeks later the screech of the brakes on the mail truck caused the head of the napping secretary to pop up from behind his typewriter. The mail carrier released the burden of letters that cascaded over his desk. Rummaging toward the bottom of the heap, the secretary came upon a letter that caught his well-trained eye. The return address was Führer's office in Berlin. This was no ordinary letter!

Suddenly the secretary realized that this letter would either bring freedom or chains to the Adventists. Quickly he open the envelope, only to find the message written in code. He reached for a pad of paper and silently translated it. Yes! It was about the Adventists in the camp!

Rocketing across the camp courtyard, he burst into the room where the Adventists were quartered—and just as suddenly he excused himself. They were praying.

They finished their prayer and looked up.

"Be glad! Be glad, Adventists! Your worries are over! Herr Himmler has sent a message saying you don't have to work on your Sabbath!"

A wave of joy swept over the group. What an answer to prayer! God had not forgotten them.

"But please," the secretary pleaded, "don't let the camp director know I've told you!"

Soon the Adventists heard that the camp director wanted to see them immediately about something important. Emma's family and friends once again stood before the camp director. He read the letter to them. "'The people in your charge are not to be molested for their religious beliefs which have brought them to their home country.'"

The camp director then said, "That was authorized by Herr Himmler, head of the Secret Police. I am glad for you. May God be praised!"

From then on the Adventists could not have had better working conditions. They had no more problems with their religion, and the camp director always referred to them as "my Adventists."

The Adventists learned that the camp director loved music. In trying to find some way to express their gratitude for the freedom of worship he had helped them obtain, the Adventists, under the direction of their tenor-voiced choir director spokesperson, organized a small singing group. That is how Emma was able to sing for the camp leader on his birthday, as well as on other special occasions.

I know this story is true, because Emma, that frightened girl back in that camp, was my mother!

14

Medals or Crowns

by Susan Carol Scharffenberg

Hey, Susan, here's a letter for you."

Pausing a moment as I typed, I reached up to take the long white envelope my sister Julie was handing me. I glanced at the return address but didn't recognize the name. Only the Mount Vernon postmark was familiar. Quickly my fingers tore the envelope open and pulled out the letter.

"Dear Susan, As coach of the Knox County Track Team, I would like to invite you to run in the A.A.U. Junior Olympics. We need some older girls to participate in this meet. Because you go to school in Knox County I thought you might like to enter the 15-17 age group. The meet will be held in Columbus on August 14, which is a Friday. I'm enclosing an application form and a list of the scheduled events. Please let me know if you are interested in entering. Sincerely, Mr. Deurieux."

"Read this, Julie!" I exclaimed.

Taking the letter from me, she scanned it hurriedly. "Sounds great! But how did he get your name?"

"Maybe he talked to Mr. Jarvis. I don't know who else would've suggested me." That seemed to be the most logical solution. Mr. Jarvis was our academy physical education teacher and knew of our interest in track.

"That's probably it," Julie agreed, "especially since we hold almost all the girls' track records at the academy."

"Too bad you'll be 18 before the meet. It would be fun if you could enter too."

I looked at the long list of events and discovered that the 880-yard run was the longest race. That would be the one for me. Here was my chance to enter a big race. My dream was coming true! I just might find my place in the world of track! As I thought of the honor and the medals that come with winning, the idea of running became even more appealing. Eagerly I filled out the application form and mailed it.

The morning of the race I awoke early, tense and excited. Dad had agreed to drive the hour journey from Kettering to Columbus. For moral support my younger sister, Barbara, and my new roommate, Joyce, went along too. When we arrived at the stadium, rows and rows of empty benches stared at us.

"Are you sure the meet is today?" Dad asked.

"Yes, I'm sure," I replied. "Maybe the time's been changed."

Sure enough, the meet had been delayed and wouldn't begin for more than an hour. My nervousness increased as I went to look for the coach.

"When do I run, Mr. Deurieux?" I asked.

"Here's a schedule of the events," he replied.

Three or four heats were scheduled for most of the events, followed by semifinals and finals. When I discovered that my event was the last one, my heart began to sink, for it was Friday. If the first events took too long, I wouldn't be able to run and would've made the trip for nothing. As the harder events were called, there were fewer contestants, so only one or two trials had to be run for each race.

Suddenly rain began to pour down, accompanied by thunder and lightning—a typical Ohio thundershower. The meet abruptly ceased as everyone ran for shelter. As I watched the raindrops form small pools of water on the track, my hopes almost died. But the shower was short-lived. A brilliant sun soon dried the track, and the meet was on.

"First call for the 880-yard run," announced one of the officials.

Only three girls had signed up for the event. *At least I can place third,* I thought. When I took my position at the starting line I learned that one of the girls had dropped out at the last minute. That meant only two of us would be running. My chances were getting better! I quickly sized up my opponent. Her long legs were no encouragement, and neither was the emblem on her red track suit, which signified that she was a member of the State team. I resolved do my best.

At the sound of the gun we were off. My long legs stretched out in an even stride, but my opponent's stride was just as long. Don't start out too fast, I cautioned myself. If you do, you'll wear out before you finish.

At the end of the first lap my opponent was in the lead. I sped up, but it was too late to catch her. Her training and experience had paid off. Not wanting to tire early, I had waited too long to close the gap and was unable to catch my opponent before she crossed the finish line. I realized I wasn't even tired.

When I went to the winner's platform to receive my silver medal, Mr. Deurieux was waiting for me. "How do you feel?" he asked.

"Full of energy!" I laughed. "Too bad this meet didn't include the mile. That's my race!"

"Your endurance is great! You look as if you could run that race all over again. Our team needs good distance runners. How would you like to try out for the State cross-country track team?"

"I'd love to. When are the tryouts?"

"Some time this fall," he replied. "If you train between now and then, I'll be able to use you on the team. We travel all over the United States for meets. You wouldn't even have to miss school, because all the meets are held on weekends."

I could hardly believe that I now had the opportunity to join the State team. Of course, it would take lots of hard work. The many hours of training would result in sore, tired muscles. But I knew I could make my dream come true if I really tried.

I was almost ready to accept the offer when I realized what Mr. Deurieux had said. The races were on weekends, which meant anytime from Friday to Sunday. "On what day are most of the events held?" I asked, hopeful that he'd say Friday or Sunday.

"Usually Saturday," he replied. "Now, I know you're a Seventh-day Adventist, but you can still run on Saturday, can't you? I'm sure your church wouldn't object under the circumstances."

I'm sure your church wouldn't object. The statement startled me. "Sir," I said, "it's not a matter of what my church thinks. It's what the Bible teaches and what I personally believe. Saturday, my Sabbath, is the day I set apart to honor God. I don't feel that I can participate in sports events held on Saturday. I wouldn't be honoring God if I did. My mind would be on personal honor and glory."

"But I'm sure it's OK," coaxed Mr. Deurieux. "By running you would be helping the team, and God wants us to help others. I've had other Adventist young people run for me here in Columbus in past years when the meet was held on Saturdays. So I know it can be arranged. You think about it and let me know your decision."

I did think about it. Why did other Adventist young people participate on Sabbath? They only made it harder for others—for me—to do what was right.

The silver medal I'd just received tempted me to try for more medals. As I fingered the glistening medal lying in the palm of my hand, I thought of the possibility of earning many more, of becoming the great runner I wanted to be.

Then I thought of another race—the one I must win—the race of life. Other young people could run on Sabbath if they chose. I was determined to win something greater than a gold medal—a golden crown presented by Christ Himself.

15

They Prayed for Rain

by Bonnie Moyers

For nearly a year Mother and her two boys, Leroy and Clinton, had been Seventh-day Adventists. Their home was much happier since Christ had come to live there. But one thing was lacking: Father was not a church member.

He often attended church with the rest of the family, and he agreed that Seventh-day Adventists were teaching the truth. "But," he insisted, "it would be impossible for me to keep the Sabbath. If I don't operate my sawmill on Saturdays, I'll lose many of my best customers. And what about this summer?"

Mother and the boys understood what he was talking about. Father's tractor, thresher, and other farm machines were in great demand during the summer. And the money he earned using the machines to help his neighbors was very important in paying the family's bills.

"I have to provide for you," Father said. "How can I do that if I turn down all Saturday work? Besides, doesn't it say somewhere in the Bible that a man should provide for his family's needs?"

So life went on without much change. If there was no work to do, Father would go to church with his family. But if someone asked Father to work on the Sabbath, he worked.

His family didn't give up easily, however. They kept right on praying that Father would change his mind. "Something is sure to happen soon," Mother said to the boys.

And it did. Mr. Jones, their next-door neighbor, came over one Friday afternoon. "Mr. Hevener," he said to Father, "I wonder if you could come over tomorrow and spread lime on my east acreage. Weather permitting, that is. The forecast calls for clear skies tomorrow."

"Certainly," Father promised. "I'll be over bright and early."

Mother overheard the entire conversation. After Mr. Jones left, she said to Father, "Did you promise Mr. Jones that you would spread lime for him tomorrow? We were so hoping you would go to church with us."

"Well, I'll go with you if it rains," was Father's answer, to which Mother replied, "Then I'm going to pray that it will rain!"

Father smiled and went on about his work.

Mother was not discouraged. When Leroy and Clinton came home from school that afternoon, she told them what had happened.

"We'll pray for rain," they decided. Three figures knelt and three heads bowed reverently as first Mother, then 12-year-old Leroy, and finally 9-year-old Clinton asked God for rain.

God heard and answered! Not immediately, but in plenty of time. The family was awakened early Sabbath morning by a steady *pitter-patter* on the roof.

Father cocked an eye open and yawned. "What's that? Rain? I won't be able to lime any fields today!"

So that Sabbath the whole family went to church together. And Mother and the boys prayed again—a prayer of thanksgiving!

All went well for about two months. Then Mr. Barrett, whose farm was five miles away, came to see Father. "Mr. Hevener," he asked Father, "could you bring your threshing machine and harvest my wheat for me tomorrow? I'll pay you well."

"Of course," Father assured him. "I'll be glad to."

"By the way," Mr. Barrett added as an afterthought, "you won't need to come if it rains. If the weather doesn't hold, I'll have to postpone threshing for a while."

If it doesn't rain. The words pricked Father like a thorn. He refused to believe that God had sent rain to keep him from liming Mr. Jones's field on the Sabbath, but the words did give him a strange feeling. When Mother learned what Mr. Barrett wanted, her face broke into a wry little smile and she said, "Guess we'll have to pray for rain again."

Once more Mother, Leroy, and Clinton fell to their knees. "Lord," they pleaded, "please do it again. Send a good rain to let Father know that he shouldn't work on Your holy day—and help him to accept You as his Savior."

Again God listened, and this time His answer was even more prompt than before. Before the family went to bed, thick dark clouds gathered, blotting out the moon. Lightning flashed and thunder pealed. Rain fell from the sky in torrents.

"Who would have thought that it would rain tonight!" exclaimed Father in astonishment. "If this gully-washer keeps on, there'll be no threshing tomorrow, that's for sure!"

The rain kept on through most of the night. Father wasn't sure whether he should be glad or sorry. But the sound of the rain was music to Mother's ears, and to Leroy's and Clinton's too. "Now you can go to church with us," they said happily.

"You didn't pray for this shower, did you?" Father asked, giving the three of them a strange look.

"We sure did," Leroy said.

"Then it must be God's doing," Father said. "I must not fight Him."

So that Sabbath the family went to church together. And from that day on, Father never missed church another Sabbath. Several months later Father was baptized.

Did Father lose anything by keeping the Sabbath? Far from it! His lumber business was very successful and more than provided for his family. He also gained the respect of his neighbors and fellow business associates. "A fine man, that Mr. Hevener," they say. "He's a good Christian who practices what he preaches."

So Father is living proof that when a man decides to do what God asks of him, God never lets him down.

The father in this story is the grandfather of the author. Leroy is her father.

16

The Church With No Name

by Dorothy Aitken

The little meetinghouse had stood there for many years. The paint was peeling. Weeds were growing in the yard. A couple of windows had been patched with cardboard. And the sign with the name of the church on it had long since disappeared. Only a few people attended services each Sabbath, and hardly anyone in town remembered that it used to be a beehive of activity, a center of religious worship for people who kept the seventh day.

On the other side of the little town lived Benedicto Bayuma. He loved to go to church. He felt clean and good and satisfied when he knelt before the high altar in the big cathedral, where the choir sang every Sunday morning and burning incense made the air smell sweet. But as he grew older he became dissatisfied. Something was lacking; what it was, he had no idea, but merely kneeling before the altar and muttering a few prayers did not satisfy him anymore.

One day Benedicto said to himself, "There are other churches in this town. Maybe I am going to the wrong one. I shall visit them all."

So Benedicto began attending all the churches in the city. Sunday after Sunday he roamed from church to church. But nothing was able to satisfy him.

"I guess there is no church that really has the answers," he decided. Feeling that God had let him down, he went back to his old life.

One night he was awakened by a strange dream. Before his eyes appeared a little old weather-beaten church. Inside he saw a man preaching. A voice said, "Here is truth."

Benedicto was so surprised that he jumped out of bed. Then he sat down on the edge of the bed and thought for a long time. Where was that church? He hadn't seen any like it anywhere in town, and he thought for sure he had visited them all by now.

One day he told a friend about his restlessness. His friend gave him a Bible. "If you love God and yet are not satisfied with the teachings of the church, maybe you should read the Bible and find out about God for yourself."

So Benedicto began to study the Bible. Soon he discovered the true Sabbath. He had no idea that anyone else in the world had ever discovered that the seventh day was the Sabbath. Surely none of the churches he had visited believed that way. So Benedicto decided that he would keep the Sabbath all by himself even if he was the only Sabbathkeeper in the whole world!

When he told his employer that he could no longer work on Saturday, Benedicto lost his job. Everywhere he applied it was the same story: Saturday was the busiest day of the week; everyone had to work on Saturday.

One day as Benedicto was waiting for a bus he met an old friend. They started talking, and Benedicto told the friend that he was out of work and could not find another job. However, he didn't tell the friend why no one would hire him.

"Look, I'm badly in need of a man to work for me," said the friend. "Why don't you come and help me out for a while? If you like it, you can stay on permanently."

Benedicto knew that he should explain about not being able to work on the Sabbath, but because he was desperate he decided not to say anything. He went home with the man and worked all week. At last it was Friday, and Benedicto was nervous. He would have to tell his kind friend that he would not be at work the next day. But how could he? He kept putting it off all day.

Finally it was closing time. Benedicto gathered up

his tools and put them away. His throat was dry. He felt miserable. Then the boss came in. "Benedicto," he said, "you won't have to come to work tomorrow."

Benedicto swallowed hard. He could not believe his ears.

"You see, Benedicto," the man went on, "the seventh day is the Sabbath of the Lord, and on that day we do not do any work. If you like, you can come again on Sunday. But if not, I'll see you on Monday."

The boss was almost gone before Benedicto could find his voice. "Señor, you keep the seventh-day Sabbath too?" Benedicto was almost hysterical with joy. "I thought I was the only one in the whole world who even knew about it."

The next day when Benedicto went to church with his employer he discovered the little weather-beaten church that had no name on the door. It was the very same church he had seen in his dream! And the preacher—he had seen him in the dream, too! Benedicto knew he had found his church at last.

When the church members heard his story they hurried to correct their mistake. The church now has a fresh coat of paint, new windows, and a name!

17

Graduation at Coquille High

by Maxine Miller

Only three weeks remained before graduation. The order blank for our announcements was to be filled out and mailed at the end of the class period. Mrs. Watson, our class advisor, stood at the front of the classroom.

"All right, class, put your books away. Bob, will you and Ray please hand out these slips of paper for me?"

The two boys went up to Mrs. Watson's desk to get the slips of paper. After each student had a slip, the teacher explained what to do.

"Now, class, write your name on the slip of paper just the way you want it printed on your name cards. Oh, and by the way, commencement exercises will be on Friday night, May 26, at 8:00."

A cold feeling went all over me as I realized what Mrs. Watson's words meant.

I had been attending Coquille High for the past four years. During those years I had been unable to attend many of the school functions, for they just about always came on Friday night or Sabbath. I wished I could go to a Seventh-day Adventist academy but the nearest one was 200 miles away and my mother couldn't afford to send me to the boarding school. I was the oldest of five children, and my stepfather wasn't interested in Christian education.

After class was over and the students had all left the room, I walked up to Mrs. Watson's desk.

"Yes, Maxine, what is it?"

"Mrs. Watson, did I hear you correctly that commencement exercises are to be on the 26th of May?"

"Yes, I just received the letter this morning from our speaker, Dr. Johnson. He has many appointments, and we are happy he has an opening that evening."

"I thought that was what you said, but I wanted to be sure." I just remained standing by her desk.

"What's wrong, Maxine?"

"Well . . ." I hesitated. "I won't be able to go to the graduation exercises. You see, I'm a Seventh-day Adventist, and we keep the Sabbath from Friday sundown to Saturday sundown. Do you think there's a chance of changing the date?"

"No, I'm very sorry, Maxine. That's the only date the speaker can come."

I was a sad girl as I boarded the school bus that afternoon. I tried to console myself with the thought that some Adventist friends of mine had had the same thing happen to them the year before and they had missed out on graduating with their class. I shook my head and decided to be brave about the whole thing.

But Mother noticed that something was wrong as soon as I entered the house. "What's wrong, dear?"

"Oh, Mom, Mrs. Watson just told us today that graduation will be on Friday night, May 26."

"Did you ask Mrs. Watson if it could be changed?"

"Yes, Mom, but there isn't a thing she can do about it." Just as I said that, an idea popped into my mind. "Mrs. Watson can't do anything about it, but God can."

So right there in the kitchen my mother knelt by the table with me, and we talked with God about my problem.

"Dear Father in heaven," my mother prayed, "You know how important graduation is to each student. Somehow make it possible that the date will be changed so Maxine may attend the exercises. In Jesus' name we ask. Your will be done. Amen."

I prayed, "Dear God, please change the date. I know You can if it is Your will. Thank You. Amen." It was a short prayer, but I felt that God could do anything.

Mom said, "I'm going to telephone Aunt Viva and write Aunt Bessie and have them pray too. I know God will make it possible for you to attend the exercises if He wants you to."

The days went by, busy busy days, as all seniors know. Our class picnic was to be held on Monday, the twenty-second of May, and there was a lot of planning and preparation. But every day, no matter how busy I was, I found time to pray my special prayer.

The commencement announcements and name cards arrived on Thursday, the eighteenth. As we were admiring them, Mrs. Watson spoke. "May I have your attention, class?"

We all looked at our adviser.

"Dr. Johnson, the speaker for our commencement exercises, just phoned a few minutes ago. It seems that there was a mistake in his appointment schedule. He already has another appointment for the night of the twenty-sixth, but he said he has an evening open, Thursday night, the twenty-fifth. You'll have to change the date on your . . ."

I didn't hear the rest of her announcement. I just bowed my head and prayed a prayer of thankfulness. "Thank You so much, dear God, for answering our prayers."

God is a loving God, I told myself, and all things are possible when you have Him on your side. Even a graduation exercise is important in His sight when you pray, believing He will answer.

"Oh," I whispered out loud, "wait until Mom hears about this."

18

The Case of the Piano Shortage

by Eunice Soper

Janet's fingers swooped up the piano keys and skittered down a long run to a crashing conclusion. Her curls bobbed as she turned her smiling face toward her teacher. "Didn't think I could ever learn that page, but I did."

"Splendid!" Mrs. Tayney applauded. "You'll have it all memorized in time for the recital."

Janet gathered up her books thoughtfully. Her teacher's recitals were really something in musical circles, and it was an honor to take part. "What day will the recital be on?" Janet remembered that in the past they generally had been on Friday night, when she couldn't attend. "You know I can't take part if it's on a Friday night or Saturday."

"Oh, yes," Mrs. Tayney brushed aside the idea with a gesture. "That's your . . . uh, 'Sabbath' you call it? Well, this will be the largest recital of the year, so I'm sure it will be all right for you to come."

Janet's head shook decidedly. "I'm afraid not, Mrs. Tayney. Not if it's on the Sabbath."

The teacher stared at her stubborn pupil for a moment before saying with a half smile, "Well, we don't have to make the decision now, do we? But you must play, for you are my most advanced pupil."

Janet couldn't help dreaming about the recital. It would be held in a big hall. Up on the platform would be 10 pianos. There would be solos, duets, and trios. But most thrilling of all would be the piano ensemble—all 10 pianos playing at once. There would be at least one big, shiny, black grand piano. And she, Janet, in her new lavender formal, would sit at it while she flawlessly played the leading part.

Down in the audience her father and mother would sit with all the other fathers and mothers. And by their shining eyes everyone would know that it was their daughter whose fingers were gliding so smoothly over the keys of the grand.

Janet would bring herself sharply from her reverie. After all, she would tell herself, the recital would probably be on the Sabbath, and she couldn't be there. Resolutely she put the dream out of her mind, but still faithfully practiced and polished her selection.

"It will be absolutely perfect by the time of the recital," Mrs. Tayney exulted one lesson period.

Janet took her courage firmly in her hands. "Mrs. Tayney, exactly when is the recital going to be held?"

Mrs. Tayney shot a quick glance at the tense face before her. "Why, the evening of May 5."

Janet's eyes darted to the calendar, and her heart sank. She had told herself that she was not planning on playing for the recital, but she could not help the sick feeling in her stomach. "I can't be there, Mrs. Tayney," she said steadily, while inside she felt like crying. "That's Friday night, part of my Sabbath. Remember, I told you about it?"

"Oh, my dear!" Mr. Tayney's face was shocked. "You simply *must* play! You are our leading pianist! We have to have you! Can't you ask your mother to please let you come to the recital?"

Tears filled Janet's eyes, and her voice trembled a bit. "Even if Mother said I could play for the recital—and I know she wouldn't do that—I couldn't. The Sabbath is God's holy day, and this is a matter between Him and me. I just couldn't attend a recital on the Sabbath."

"Well, we simply can't have it at another time," Mrs. Tayney spoke a bit sharply. "I don't believe the hall will be available any other time. And that is the only time we will be able to get that many pianos at one time."

"I don't expect you to change the date for me," said Janet, "but I can't be there on the Sabbath."

Janet left the studio with a feeling of deep discouragement. She had worked so hard on her piece. And she did want to have a part in the big recital. Subsequent lessons did not help much either, for each week Mrs. Tayney tried to coax her into playing, and each week Janet had to explain again that she could not play on the Sabbath.

Weeks went by. Janet practiced faithfully until she could play her piece faultlessly. Finally it was time for the last lesson before the great recital day.

Mrs. Tayney met her stubborn pupil at the door. "Janet, you win!" she exclaimed happily. "We're going to have the recital on Thursday night instead of Friday night."

The startled girl's eyes widened unbelievingly. "What—what do you mean?"

"Simply that there is not a piano available in all Kansas City for use on Friday night. *Not a single one!* But I can have all I want on Thursday night. I just don't understand it. I've never had so much trouble renting pianos!" She sounded bewildered and just a little annoyed. "And the hall is available on Thursday night, too."

Relief, wonder, joy, and gratitude sped over Janet's countenance, wiping away all the uncertainty of the past weeks. "Oh, I'm so glad I know my piece" was all she said aloud. But her heart said, "Thank You, thank You, thank You, Lord!"

19

Trial by Firing Squad

as told to Marvin Moore

I stood in the gravel pit by the pump house, shovel in hand and the words of refusal still on my lips. The sergeant's voice shook with anger.

"Either you shovel that pile of gravel, or my firing squad shoots!" He clenched his fist in my face. "We teach soldiers to obey orders seven days a week in this Army!"

The knots in my stomach tightened. The sergeant whirled and marched straight to his rifle squad. My frantic mind clawed for some clue that this was not the end, that he was only bluffing. The crescents his heels chopped in the hot summer dirt didn't give me any encouragement. He barked an order, then whirled again. His arm flew up, and a pudgy finger pointed straight at my face.

My fingers tightened around the shovel. I waited,

eyes clamped shut, ears tensed for him to bark the last words I ever expected to hear. Then heavy footsteps pounded back toward me. I dared my eyes open and wished I hadn't.

Shoot! Shoot! my mind screamed.

He moved in, eyeball-to-eyeball. Beads of sweat on his forehead dripped onto mine. I felt his heart pound. His tobacco-stained breath blasted the order. "Soldier! Move that shovel!" Then he backed off and glared.

My brain whirled. Confusion fogged me in. "God," I breathed. And then I knew what I had to do. I held the shovel out to him. "Shoot me if you wish," I said, "but I cannot do what you ask."

His jaw dropped. Disbelief broke through the rage on his face. Fire seemed to shoot out of his eyes as they met mine for a brief second. He turned to his men and sent them on their way with a crisp "Dismissed!" Then he bellowed, "Soldier, the CO wants to see you at 16:00 at headquarters. Now get to your barracks!"

After what seemed an endless walk past taunts and jeers of "holy-day boy" and "Advent Sabbathkeeper," I finally reached the barracks. I sank down on my bunk, relieved to be alone in the empty room. "God," I cried, "where are You? You worked everything out so perfectly last week. How did all this happen?"

To the Adventist evangelist who baptized me on a Sabbath morning late in 1916, the World War was mainly a sign of the end. Few Americans felt personally involved. Hadn't our president promised to keep us out of war? Then suddenly we were very much involved. I obeyed my summons to serve, wondering just how my new faith would fit in with Uncle Sam's Army.

But God was on my side. Without speaking to a single officer about my Sabbath, I had simply prayed and hoped. And God had honored my trust. Early that first Sabbath morning an officer had called us all out to the parade grounds for a surprise inspection. One bold exception stood out among the wrinkled batch of GIs that straggled out and lined up: me!

"One thing you men had better learn in this Army and fast!" the officer scolded. "You are *always* ready for inspection. Out of this whole company only one man is ready. Congratulations, Cleveland. You may take the day off. Pick up a pass at headquarters. The rest of you report for work at 9:00!"

The poor officer was quite unaware that I had prepared for church, *not* for his inspection. What a God! With Him on my side, Army life would be a snap!

But now this. I sat on my cot and tried to think through the events of this second Sabbath morning. I searched for an answer, but like a whirlpool my dazed brain sucked every snatch of hope out of reach.

I turned to lie down, and my face brushed against something. As I pushed it aside, I realized that it was my Bible. I sat up and turned to the story of Daniel in the lions' den. Then with new courage I leafed back to the Psalms. "Call upon me in the day of trouble; I will deliver you, and you will honor me" (Psalm 50:15). I sank to my knees to claim God's promise.

A moment later I heard loud, explosive talk coming my way. I tensed and jumped to my feet when a voice spoke up. "That'll teach him to spruce up for his Sabbath and put us to work all day while he goes out and has a lark. By the time we get through giving him a sand bath he won't be sitting, standing, or lying for a week!"

With the Bible open on the cot in front of me, I stayed on my knees, my head bowed, my eyes closed. Feet hit the front steps and the door flew open. In stomped a half dozen soldiers. I knew they could hardly wait to get their hands on me.

The room became deathly silent. For a moment, not a man moved. I heard whispers. Then they left the barracks on tiptoe.

Now I knew how Mary Magdalene must have felt when her accusers walked away. I realized that God was still on my side. I had been spared a rubdown with sand by men so angry they would have left my body one solid abrasion. After a prayer of thanksgiving I sat down again and searched for Bible texts to memorize in preparation for my interview with the commanding officer.

I stepped into the headquarters building a few

hours later, Bible in hand. A private pecked at a typewriter on a desk in the middle of the room. He stopped long enough to hear my name and motion me to a chair. I sat down beside what I concluded must be the door to the commander's office.

Across the room hung a framed picture of President Woodrow Wilson. Under the windows along the back wall stood two wooden tables and an antique filing cabinet. A clock between the windows announced the time: 3:45. I had purposely arrived a few minutes early.

I settled back to wait. A strange new peace settled over me. Gone was the fog, the confusion of the morning. I sat there for several minutes, eyes shut, praying. Then the commanding officer's door flew open and out burst two distraught junior officers. I jerked my feet in as they rushed past. The commander, Major Stanfield, strode out the door after them.

"Where's Cleveland!" he demanded. Anger edged his voice. "Isn't it enough he disobeyed orders this morning without being late to see me? Get him here!" he ordered.

Glancing up, the private nodded in my direction. "He's right over there, sir."

Major Stanfield turned and glared at me. "Soldier," he barked, "don't you know that 16:00 means 4:00? Look at that clock, and next time be here three minutes early!"

I looked. The clock said 3:57. "Yes, sir," I mumbled, and stepped into his office.

The commander followed me in, stepped behind his large mahogany desk, and sat down. On the wall above him hung a picture of the president, flanked by two flags.

He motioned to a chair in front of the desk. "Sit there."

I sat down. After a long period of silence, he shifted in his chair. "Cleveland," he growled, "they tell me you disobeyed orders this morning and talked back to a noncommissioned officer. What do you have to say for yourself?" He leaned his large swivel chair back, eyeing me through a haze of cigar smoke.

"The sergeant told me to shovel gravel on my Sabbath, sir." I wondered whether my waning courage or my jitters showed through more. "But I was not aware of talking back. I'm sorry if I did."

Major Stanfield leaned forward again. His eyes glared into mine. "In this Army, Cleveland, any time you refuse to obey an order you're talking back. And as for Sabbath-keeping, this is the Army, not church. We don't know what that Sabbath of yours is all about, and what's more, we aren't interested in finding out."

He paused, reached for a pen and paper, and began to write. After a line or two he looked up. "No, young man," he continued, his voice slightly softer, "I'm not going to do anything about this morning's incident. But next Saturday morning you'd better do what you're told or you'll be in for real trouble. Is that clear?"

"God, what do I say now?" I breathed. The story of the three Hebrews before the enraged Nebuchadnezzar flashed across my mind. I looked up. "Sir, I understand what you said and why you said it. But I cannot work on God's Sabbath. It begins at sundown on Friday and ends at sundown on Saturday. I'll be glad to do double duty any other time. But it will be impossible for me to work on the Sabbath."

Eyes glaring through slits, the commander half rose from his chair. His face reddened. Jaw set, he leaned toward me. His tight fist slammed the table.

"Soldier," he growled, "what kind of Army do you think this would be if every man here told us what he was and wasn't going to do, and when he planned to do it? Next Friday night, or Saturday morning, or whenever it is, you'll do what you're told!" He shook his head violently.

"Sir, it's not that I won't. I can't. My Bible teaches me that God's law is above every human law, and the Sabbath is one of His laws. I must obey God."

Major Stanfield settled back into his chair. "Private Cleveland," he said tersely, "you're under company arrest. Report to this office for court martial in three days, at this same time. Till then, stay in your barracks. That is all." He rose, motioning toward the door.

I stood to leave.

He stepped to the door and reached for the handle, then turned and faced me again. "Your meals will be brought to you," he said. "And bring along that book with your laws in it when you come back."

Three days later I sat in the commander's waiting room once again. Pictures of the past two weeks drifted through my mind. I thought of God's answer to prayer that first Sabbath morning in the Army that gave me the day off without me even having to ask for it. I thought of the sergeant's terrifying bluff before a "firing squad" the past Sabbath and of the deliverance God gave me from a torturous sand bath a few minutes later. I thought of the tense interview with Commander Andrew Stanfield and the past three days of Bible study and prayer, preparing for this afternoon's court-martial.

It began to dawn on my mind that perhaps the Lord was answering my prayer for freedom to keep His Sabbath holy, but in a different way. After all, I was still very much alive. I hadn't been sent to the guardhouse. They had trusted me to stay in my own quarters and to appear on time for the court-martial without sending a military policeman to escort me.

"Lord, I don't know what they'll do to me in there," I prayed, "but I trust you to give me the right words to say. Help me—"

Heavy footsteps interrupted my prayer. I heard joking and laughing. Seconds later the front door opened, and several officers and a sergeant, severe looks now on their faces, stepped to the private's desk.

The private and I jumped to attention and saluted.

"We are here to see Major Stanfield for a court-martial," a heavyset captain announced.

"Major Stanfield said he would see you as soon as you arrive, sir." The private stepped to the door and knocked. After a pause he entered. Seconds later he emerged and addressed the captain. "The commander says he'll be with you in just a minute, sir."

"I hope he won't be too long," the lieutenant snapped. "I haven't got all day for this affair."

"You may be seated if you wish, sir," the private said. "He's just signing a few documents."

The lieutenant took the chair next to mine, then edged away from me. I felt like poison. The others stood, blowing cigarette smoke around the room.

The front door burst open again, and another lieutenant hurried in. He puffed and wiped his face. "What's this hearing all about, anyway?" he shot at the captain. "They called me at the last minute, and I'm stacked to the gills with reports to get to Washington by Monday. I suppose this'll make me one more." He shot an icy glance my way.

"Sir, some recruit thinks he's going to baptize the

U.S. Army into his church," spat out an all-too-familiar voice.

Jarred out of what little composure I had left, I recognized the bullying sergeant I'd met at the gravel pile three days before. He flipped a cigarette into an ashtray.

Just then Major Stanfield stepped out of his office. The lieutenant next to me snapped to his feet. The others and I joined him in a smart salute. The commander touched his fingers to his forehead and motioned toward the door.

"We'll call for you when we're ready, Cleveland," Major Stanfield said. He turned and closed the door behind him.

I waited for what seemed an eternity. When the door opened again, I heard the sergeant's order. "Private Cleveland, Major Stanfield wants to see you in here!"

I picked up my Bible, stepped past the sergeant into the room, and saluted. Behind the desk sat the five men who were to hear my case.

"Be seated, Private Cleveland." Major Stanfield waved toward the chair I had occupied three days earlier. I felt like the proverbial sheep among wolves as I sat down facing the men.

The major cleared his throat. "Private Cleveland, this is Captain Smith and Lieutenant Carter on my left, and Lieutenant Hurst and Sergeant Spears on my right."

I exchanged glances with the officers.

"We understand," Stanfield continued, "that at 0900 hours last Saturday morning, you refused to obey Sergeant Spears' order to work at the gravel pile by the pump house. Give an account of yourself."

"I'm happy to obey any order I'm given by a—"

"By a supervisor you feel like obeying!" interrupted the sergeant.

"Cleveland!" Captain Smith burst out. "Either you get that crazy religion out of your head, or you'll be serving this Army a whole lot longer than you imagined."

"Sir," I replied, "my religion teaches me to obey my government's superiors. And that includes officials in the Army. However, my religion also teaches me to—"

"Listen, soldier," cut in Lieutenant Hurst, "we haven't got all day to listen to you preach about your church. You're making me have to fill out one more report to send to Washington, as if that's all I had to do. Will you do what you are told, when you are told? That's all Washington wants to know, and that's all I care to waste the ink to tell them!"

"Cleveland, you may finish what you have to say," broke in Major Stanfield. "We will listen." He leaned back in his chair and puffed on his cigar.

"Thank you, sir," I replied. "As I said, I do not wish to disobey my superiors. But as a Christian, I believe I must obey God rather than human authority any time the two conflict. The Bible teaches that Saturday is the Sabbath and forbids work on that day. That is why I could not do what Sergeant Spears ordered me to do last Saturday morning."

"Soldier," the captain harangued, "what outfit taught you this nonsense, anyway? Were your parents foolish enough to raise you this way?"

"No, sir," I replied. "I have believed this for less than a year. I am a Seventh-day Adventist. I—"

"A seven-day how many?" Lieutenant Carter queried.

"Seventh-day Adventist," Major Stanfield volunteered. He picked up a card and leaned toward Lieutenant Carter. "It's right here on his record. Go ahead, Cleveland." He handed the card to the other officer.

"I joined this church of my own free will after hearing a series of Bible lectures in my hometown. I realize the problem I'm causing, and I wish it didn't have to be this way. But I believe with all my heart that Saturday is the Sabbath, and I'm prepared to take the consequences, even if it means death."

"That's the ridiculous truth!" muttered the sergeant, half under his breath. His eyes met mine— the same flashing eyes I'd seen the previous Sabbath morning at the gravel pit.

"I really don't care where you got this notion or

who put it into your head," Captain Smith spat out, "but I know who's going to get it out!"

"I wouldn't be too sure of that, sir," Spears growled. "You should have seen the idiot make a fool of himself last Saturday morning—excuse me, Private, Sabbath morning," he added in mock respect.

There was a pause. Tension filled the room. My stomach convulsed. I held my breath and tightened my muscles.

"Your church teaches you to rebel against the government?" exploded Lieutenant Carter. "Rebellion! That's all it is. Rebellion, pure and simple!" He half stood and pointed his finger at me. "Maybe you will die before this is settled! Die over some foolish notion!"

I looked at my feet. Silently I asked God for help. I decided there wasn't anything I could do by myself. So I sat there with my head bowed.

Major Stanfield broke the silence. "Gentlemen," he said, rising to his feet, "I think Private Cleveland's position is quite clear to all of us. That is what I wanted you to hear. I will have to think this case through some more before I decide what to do. I know you are all busy with other responsibilities. You may be excused."

The four rose to leave. The commander moved around his desk and stepped to open the door. "Lieutenant Carter," he said, "I'll make out the report on this incident myself."

"Yes, sir; thank you, sir," replied the lieutenant. The three officers and the sergeant saluted smartly and left the room. I leaned forward to stand, but Major Stanfield stopped me with a wave of his hand.

The door closed again; Major Stanfield returned to his chair behind the desk. I felt his searching look fixed on me. I glanced at him out of the corner of my eye and wondered what he was thinking. His face looked serious, but he didn't seem angry. He sat for several minutes, scarcely moving. He thoughtfully rubbed his chin with his fingers.

Presently he got up. Taking Sergeant Spears' chair, he brought it around the desk and set it down close to mine.

"Cleveland," he said, "the Army isn't opposed to men going to church on Sunday from time to time. You want it on Saturday. I think that could be arranged. But you're different. You insist that it's got to be every Saturday. And not just for services in the morning, but for the whole day, starting on Friday night! I told you to bring that book with you when you came to see me this afternoon. Now I want you to show me from the Bible where it says that."

With a prayer that the Lord would guide me, I began with the story of Creation. Moving through to the experience of the children of Israel, I explained the fourth commandment and the sacredness of the day. I pointed out God's intention of blessing a specific day, as seen in His own miracle of the manna for 40 years. In the New Testament I pointed out the example of Christ and the apostles. The commander's interest seemed genuine. I concluded with the prophecy about Sabbath-keeping in the new earth in the last chapters of Isaiah.

"Young man, I can see you know what you believe. I'd like to know what you people have to say about war."

With another prayer for help, I did the best I could to explain. When we finished with war, he wanted to know about the second coming of Christ. Then about death, the resurrection, the judgment, the millennium, and hell. The kind of questions he asked gave me the distinct impression that he knew more about Seventh-day Adventists than he cared to reveal, and that he was testing me to see what I knew. We sat for an hour, covering nearly every phase of the church's beliefs. With each passing moment his attitude became more favorable.

Finally, when Major Stanfield stood to his feet, I did too. He put out his hand. "Cleveland, I congratulate you on knowing so well what you believe. For one so recently baptized into your faith, I am amazed at your knowledge. I know all about Seventh-day Adventists. They're good people. My family hires a Seventh-day Adventist maid, and she gives us honest, faithful service. Don't worry about that report to

Washington. It will be favorable. And don't worry about your Sabbath, either. As long as you are under my command, the time is yours from sundown Friday till sundown Saturday."

Relief flooded over me. I felt weak, but I mustered the courage to salute and say, "Yes, sir; thank you, sir!"

The officer walked with me to the door and held it open. "Oh, one other thing." He touched my arm to stop me. There was a twinkle in his eye. "Mind you, don't go teaching that religion of yours around here too much, or we won't have any Army left!"

He gave me a gentle push out the door.

20

God Worked Things Out

by Bonnie Moyers

Dietrich Mueller was a German boy with loving parents, a good home, and kind neighbors. One of the neighbors, Mrs. Schmidt, lived across the street. Nine-year-old Dietrich noticed that she left her house every Saturday wearing her best clothes. One day Dietrich asked Mrs. Schmidt, "Where do you go every Saturday morning when you leave the house all dressed up?"

Mrs. Schmidt smiled at Dietrich. "If you really want to know, I'll tell you. Every Saturday morning I go to church."

"Church?" Dietrich couldn't believe his ears. All his friends went to church on Sunday like he did. "You go to church on Saturday? What kind of church has meetings on Saturday?"

"The Seventh-day Adventist Church. Every

Saturday morning our church has Sabbath school at 9:30 and church service at 11:00. We have special programs for people of all ages. You would enjoy the things the children do in the primary division."

"What sort of things do they do?" Dietrich wanted to know.

"Fun things," Mrs. Schmidt explained. "In Sabbath school you would hear interesting stories. And I'm sure you would enjoy the songs they sing. They also play Bible games and have quizzes."

"That does sound like fun," Dietrich agreed. "Could I go with you when you go to church this week?"

"If your parents say it's all right for you to go," Mrs. Schmidt promised, "I'll gladly take you with me."

When Sabbath came, Dietrich was dressed in his best suit and his face was so clean that it shone. He and Mrs. Schmidt slipped into her little Volkswagen and away they went to the Adventist church.

Dietrich decided right away that he liked the looks of the neat brick church building with the evergreen shrubbery nestled around it and the well-kept lawn. And the people were friendly. A boy about his age moved over on the bench so Dietrich had a place to sit. Dietrich enjoyed everything. Sabbath school really was fun!

During the church service the pastor told the children a story about the trouble a little boy got into when he didn't obey his parents. Then he told them that they could listen in on the grown people's sermon if they wished. Dietrich decided that he would listen in, and he was pleased that he could make sense of almost everything the pastor said.

On the way home he told Mrs. Schmidt, "I really enjoyed going to your church today. Could I come back with you again sometime?"

"Of course you may."

"Did you enjoy your visit to the Adventist church?" Dietrich's mother asked when he stepped inside the door.

"Yes, I did—very much."

"What did you learn today?" his father asked.

"One thing I learned was that boys and girls should pay attention to what their parents say—that parents usually know what's best for them."

"That was a worthwhile thing to learn, son," Father agreed. "I'm glad you went to church. It's better than some other places you could go."

So it was that the very next week when Dietrich asked permission to go to Sabbath school, the answer was, "Yes, you may go."

The weeks lengthened into months and years, and Dietrich attended Sabbath school and church every week. He was now 14 years old. He knew he loved Jesus with all his heart. One Sabbath when Pastor Heinrich asked those who wanted to give their hearts to God, be baptized, and join the

Seventh-day Adventist Church to stand and come to the front of the church, Dietrich was on his feet at once. The baptism would take place in two weeks.

But when Dietrich told his parents that he had decided to be baptized into the Adventist Church, his father shouted, "You've got to be crazy!"

"Why do you say that?" Dietrich was puzzled at his father's reaction, because he had not seemed to mind his attending the Adventist Church all these years.

"I say that because if you become an Adventist and keep Saturday when the rest of the world keeps Sunday, you will have all kinds of trouble getting work or setting yourself up in business. You will be so different from everybody else. It's not worth your while."

"I'm not worried about whether or not I can get work," Dietrich tried to explain. "What's more important than what kind of job I get is that I must do what I feel is right. I love God with all my heart and believe that the best way I can serve Him is by joining the Seventh-day Adventist Church."

Mother looked sad. "But couldn't you serve God just as well in our church?" she wanted to know.

Before Dietrich could answer her question, his father pulled a stack of bank notes from his pocket. Holding them out toward Dietrich, he said, "Son, let's be reasonable about this. See all this money? I'm a wealthy man. I'll give you all this money and more if you'll forget about joining the Adventist Church.

With this money, you could be almost anything you want to be in life. I could help you get set up in the business of your choice. Here—the money is yours."

But Dietrich answered, "I'm sorry, but I can't take it."

His father's face turned an angry red. "Don't bother to come home after your baptism. Pack your clothes and take them with you the day you are baptized. For after that day, this will no longer be your home. And I will no longer think of you as my son!"

Dietrich's mother sat silently. Tears filled her eyes and spilled onto her cheeks. She didn't want Dietrich to leave home, but what could she do or say? She was afraid to go against what her husband had said.

"I'm sorry things have to be like this," Dietrich replied. "But if I must choose between serving God and having a future in big business, then I choose God."

In the two weeks that followed, nothing changed. Dietrich's father still said he must leave home if he went through with being baptized. Sadly, Dietrich packed his clothing and prepared to leave. Sabbath morning dawned bright and clear. And although Dietrich knew he couldn't come back home after the baptismal service, he still had peace in his heart. He felt sure that he was doing the right thing. As he was getting ready for the baptism, he talked with Pastor Heinrich.

"Yes, you really do have a problem," the pastor

agreed. "If you were full grown and trained to do some special kind of work, you could find a job and your troubles would be pretty well over. But you're only 14. However, you can stay at our house until we work something out for you."

After much thought, prayer, and earnest talk, it was decided that Dietrich should attend the Seventh-day Adventist academy in Cologne. There he could work his way through school by working around the campus and in the classrooms.

Dietrich went to the academy, and he loved the school with its Christian teachers. But although his Sabbathkeeping problems were over, his money problems had just begun. He was penniless when he left home, and the wages he earned by doing janitorial and maintenance work and grading papers for teachers were not very high. Dietrich realized that in order to pay his bills so he could remain in school, he could eat only one meal a day and none on Sabbath.

Poor Dietrich! He would skip breakfast and lunch and eat supper, so he wouldn't have to go to bed feeling hungry. It was hard, studying and working all day on an empty stomach. Many times Dietrich felt so weak and tired that he had to force his weary arms and legs to keep going until all his work was done.

Sabbaths were worst of all. Dietrich's stomach growled all through Sabbath school and church. It pained him all through special Sabbath afternoon activities and vespers. Hardest of all was trying to go to sleep on Saturday nights. Those gnawing hunger pangs were almost more than Dietrich could stand.

Dietrich could have told his roommate or some of his teachers about his plight. But he didn't. His roommate had all he could do to earn his own way through school. And he felt that his teachers were already doing all they could to help him.

One Sabbath morning Dietrich woke up hungry as usual. As he counted the money he had set aside for tithe, a thought came to him. "You've got so much money there. Why don't you borrow some of it and buy yourself a good breakfast for a change? It would be all right if you paid it back later on."

Throwing himself on the bed, Dietrich cried in his despair, "Oh, Jesus, You know how hungry I am. You were hungry Yourself when the devil tempted You in the wilderness. But You didn't give in. Please help me not to. I'm so hungry I feel like I'm going to faint. Thank You, Jesus. Amen."

Dietrich wiped his eyes and dressed for church. He had no way of knowing it then, but not only had God heard his heartfelt prayer but help was already on its way. He went to Sabbath school and church as usual and turned his tithe in. Shortly after the offering plate was passed, a deacon tapped Dietrich on the shoulder and whispered, "Someone wants to see you in the hall."

Dietrich stepped out into the hall. There stood a messenger with a special delivery letter. "A letter for you—special delivery. Please sign that you received it."

Dietrich signed for the letter, and the messenger left. The handwriting was familiar. The letter was from his mother. He hadn't heard from his mother or father since the day he had left home several months before. Was it bad news inside the letter? He opened it with trembling hands. As he did so, a check for $1,500 fell out. "Dear Son," the letter read, "Regardless of what your father said, I still love you and care about what happens to you. To me you are still my son. I know it costs a lot of money to attend boarding school, and I hope this check will help defray your expenses. Lovingly, Mother."

Fifteen hundred dollars! That was more, much more money than he had ever dared hope for. Now he had enough money to take him the rest of the way through academy. He could buy clothing. And he could get enough to eat—three square meals a day. A very happy Dietrich thanked God for answering his prayer so promptly as he sat down with his friends in the cafeteria to enjoy the first good Sabbath dinner he had been able to have since he had first arrived at the school.

Dietrich went on to college and is now serving God as a minister. He will never forget how God answered his prayer when he needed an answer so desperately.

21

Tiago and the Six-Foot Fish

by Marvin Moore

Tiago's hand clutched the front of the rowboat on both sides. The salt air blew his long, black hair into his face. He brushed the strands aside.

Pushing the toes of his right foot into the bottom of the boat, Tiago leaned over the edge and peered into the clear water below. Behind him his father leaned hard on a long pole that was stuck in the sandy ocean floor, keeping the boat just far enough away from a net on the left to give the boy a good view of any fish that might be caught in its webbing.

Tiago turned and looked at his father. The muscles in the boy's arms tightened, and he clenched his fists. "We have to keep going!" he exclaimed.

Man and boy looked at each other for a brief moment. Then the man turned and studied the sun that dipped toward the village behind him. Looking back at the boy, he hesitated a second. "OK, for just a bit longer," he said.

Tiago whirled, bent over the edge again, and gazed into the water. His back glistened in the sun. The ocean waves slapped the side of the boat and spattered a crazy pattern of splotches across his cut-off khakis. An inch of water sloshed across the floor as the boat bobbed up and down. A rope lay coiled in the bottom, its frayed end tied to a long spear that rolled with the movement of the boat. A hunting knife lay beside it.

The boy kept his eyes fixed on the net in the water below. The man turned now and again to look at the sun. "We have to stop," he said at last, half rising to his feet. The boy shook his head and leaned farther over the edge.

"Tiago!" the man ordered. He stood and moved toward the boy.

Tiago bolted to his feet, violently rocking the boat. "A fish!" he yelled.

The man caught his balance and moved swiftly to his son's side. Together they leaned over the edge. In the clear water they saw a fish about six feet long caught by the gills in the web of the net.

Tiago seized the spear. "You keep it from getting away," he said, and handed the coil of rope to his father. Then he leaned over the side again, grasped the spear high over his head, and hurled it at the fish.

When the fish rested quietly, Tiago dived into the sea, untangled it from the net, and helped his father load it into the boat.

Ten minutes later a half dozen fishermen crowded around as Tiago and his father landed their boat and lifted their catch onto the sand.

"A good omen! A good omen!" exclaimed an old man, slightly stooped, but a strong fisherman still. He moved a bushy eyebrow up and down as he spoke. Diaglo was the village sage, prophet, and priest. "Soon we will all catch fish!" he said.

"Nacimento, you are a lucky man!" one of them said, slapping Tiago's father hard across the back. "And you still have three hours left before dark to catch more. Soon you will be the richest of us all!"

Tiago's father glanced at the sun, then turned to his friend and smiled. "No, Amorim," he said, removing his hat and brushing his thinning hair with his hand. "I must take this one home now and prepare for the Sabbath. God gave me this fish, and I must not dishonor Him by working on His Sabbath."

Amorim's jaw dropped. He stared a moment, then turned to leave. "Stupid!" he muttered to himself as he walked away.

A murmur ran through the group of fishermen still gathered around the big fish. One by one they returned to their own nets.

Tiago watched them leave. His jaws tightened, and

he glared at his father. He drew a deep breath and let it out slowly. "Let's go," he said quietly. And he dropped to his knees and picked the fish up by the head.

Alexandre Nacimento and his wife, Nazare, had joined the Seventh-day Adventist Church about a year before. Two of their children had been baptized too, but even before his baptism, Tiago, the oldest son, had chafed under what he called "those dumb rules."

A severe economic depression had struck their small fishing village on the northeastern coast of Brazil shortly after the Nacimento family became Adventists. For several months now nobody had caught more than enough small fish to survive. The large fish that brought high profits seemed to be a thing of the past—until today.

The houses in the village flanked either side of a narrow, winding street about a quarter of a mile up from the seashore. Tiago and his father carried their fish up the beach to the family's thatch-roofed house. The younger children danced about when the two fishermen entered their home with the day's catch. Alexandre urged everyone to prepare for the Sabbath, while his wife and their oldest daughter cleaned the fish in the small lean-to kitchen behind the house.

Toward evening, Alexandre stepped outside and checked the western sky. "Mother! Tiago! Children!" he called. "The Sabbath is coming. It's time for sundown worship."

Nazare came into the front room from the kitchen and sat beside her husband in a double wicker chair. On a low table in front of them were a large family Bible, a small tin can with a wick that poked up from a hole in the top, and a box of matches. The younger children came—some from the family bedroom, some from their play outside—and sat in smaller chairs or on the floor around the table.

Alexandre picked up the Bible. He turned the pages to find a text, then glanced about the room. He frowned. "Tiago!" he called.

Tiago shuffled into the room and sat on the floor, cross-legged, his chin in his hands. He kept his eyes fixed on a red ant that crawled up and down a leg of the table. "Dumb!" he kept muttering softly to himself.

Just as his father was about to read from the Bible, Tiago heard footsteps running up to their house. A second later he heard a loud knock at the door. "Nacimento! Nacimento!" a voice called. Tiago recognized the voice. It was Amorim, the fisherman who had disgustedly walked away on the beach several hours before.

Tiago leaped to his feet, threw the door open, and Amorim stepped inside. Amorim looked at Alexandre, who still sat in the wicker chair, Bible in hand. "There's another huge fish in your net!" Amorim exclaimed. "If you hurry, you can still get it before dark. I can take you right to it and help you bring it in."

Alexandre Nacimento rose slowly from his chair and walked over to his friend. He placed a hand on Amorim's shoulder and looked into his eyes before he spoke. "Thank you for telling me," he said with a smile. "But it is already the Lord's Sabbath, and I cannot go out."

"But it may get away! Somebody may steal it!" Amorim retorted. "Besides, Diaglo said it would be an ill omen for all of us if it escapes."

"God can take care of it," Alexandre said. "If He wants me to have it, it will still be there tomorrow night."

"But . . ."

Tiago saw the fire in Amorim's eyes. He watched the crimson around his shirt collar as it rose and covered his face. He heard the words as they burst from Amorim's lips. "Stupid!" he hissed in front of the whole family before turning and stalking through the door.

Alexandre closed the door, sighed, and returned to his seat beside his wife. Tiago saw her squeeze his hand in hers as he sat down. His father turned and smiled at her, then opened the Bible and began to read.

Tiago scarcely heard a word. God, money, the Sabbath, work. The thoughts raced about and crossed one another in his mind.

"Father, it doesn't make sense!" he blurted.

His father laid the Bible in his lap and looked at Tiago.

"What doesn't make sense?" he asked.

"That we're all about to starve, but we can't work because of some rule that says not to. If that fish weren't there, it would be different, but it is there!" He turned toward the window and motioned with his hand toward the darkening sky outside.

Tiago watched as his father reached over to the table and took a match from the box. Striking it against the leather sole of his shoe, he held it to the wick in the can until the primitive lamp cast a bright light about the room.

"Son," he said, "I'm glad to see that you're a hard worker. You will be successful in life, I know."

Tiago felt a touch of pride and sat a bit straighter.

"God has commanded us to work," his father continued. "But He has given us some guidelines to follow. Six days are ours; the seventh belongs to Him. If we really want to succeed, we must do our work His way, not ours. He made us, you know." The man turned his face up, and their eyes met.

Tiago looked away and shifted on the floor. A moment later he stood to his feet. "I don't know. I just don't know!" he said, and he turned and stumbled back into his bedroom.

Unfolding his hammock, Tiago stretched it between two hooks in the ceiling and curled up in it. From the living room he heard low voices. Twice he thought he heard his name. He knew when the family knelt to pray. His father always spoke in a lower, more distinct voice when he prayed. Again he heard his name.

Tiago was only vaguely aware of the other family members when they entered the bedroom a half hour later and stretched out in their own hammocks. He slept fitfully all night. Once, when he opened his eyes, he saw the eerie shadows of the moon through a tall banana tree outside the window. Toward morning he fell into a deeper sleep and dreamed of piles and piles of huge fish in the sand on the beach.

After breakfast and a short worship the next morning, the entire family set out for church. The younger children skipped and ran ahead. Tiago hung back.

Services were held in the small front room of the deacon's home. Tiago waited outside for the singing to end before going in. Each Sabbath morning the deacon hung a sign on the gray mud wall beside his front door announcing the services in bold, crudely shaped letters. But few people attended, other than the handful of regular members. "Church in that little rathole?" Tiago had heard his friends chuckle.

As three of the members were shaking Tiago's hand at the door, Amorim and Diaglo trudged down the street toward the beach, dragging a newly repaired length of fishnet between them. Tiago caught a brief glance from Diaglo as they passed by. Diaglo muttered something, and both men shook their heads.

"Tiago! Tiago!"

Tiago whirled. Two boys and a girl were racing down the street toward him.

"Tiago!" panted the taller boy as he slowed to a trot, then stopped. "My father said you caught two fish in your trap yesterday!"

"Yes." Tiago stared at the dust on the ground and kicked a pebble with his toe.

"How much do they weigh?"

"I don't know," Tiago replied. "We brought only one of them in, and we didn't weigh it because it was too late."

"Too late?"

"Yes, too near the Sabbath. My father won't let us do any work on the Sabbath."

"But what about the other fish?"

"We didn't find out about it till it was too late," Tiago replied. "We haven't gone after it yet."

"You what?"

Tiago glanced at his friend out of the corner of his eye and nodded, then kicked the pebble again.

"I'm sure glad my father doesn't make us go to this dumb old church," the girl snickered.

The trio stood around awkwardly for a few seconds. "Well, have a nice Sabbath, Tiago," one of the boys sneered, and they raced on down the street toward the beach.

Tiago slipped into a chair near the back just as the deacon was offering the opening prayer. "And help us to find the money to build a new church in this village so that we can better honor Your name. Amen." was all Tiago heard.

"Dumb!" he muttered under his breath. "If people would use their heads, they'd soon have the money for a church."

Tiago sat through most of the service with his elbows on his knees, his chin in his hands, his eyes fixed on the floor. He hurried home at noon, hoping none of his friends would see him. All afternoon he stayed in the house.

"And if You have kept the fish for us over the Sabbath," his father prayed as they knelt at the close of sundown worship, "help us to find it before it gets too dark. Thank You for answering our prayer. In Jesus' name we pray. Amen."

Tiago drew a deep breath as they rose from their knees.

"Change your clothes quickly," his father said. "I believe God will answer our prayer."

Down at the beach 15 minutes later, Tiago and father dragged their boat to the water. Several curious villagers watched from a distance.

Amorim sauntered up. "Well," he said. A note of ridicule tinged the skepticism in his voice. "Do you *really* think it will be there?"

"If God wants it to be."

"Humph!" Amorim grunted. "Well, it was about halfway to the end of your net." He motioned toward a float that bobbed at the end of Alexandre's net, some distance out from the shore.

Tiago leaped into the boat after his father.

"Watch that knife, son," Alexandre said as Tiago crossed to the front of the boat. "You almost stepped on it with your bare feet."

Tiago glanced at the knife that lay beside the spear and the coiled rope in the bottom of the boat, then took his place at the front, peering only casually over the edge into the clear water below. His father strained at the pole to move the boat as rapidly as possible. Tiago glanced into the water again.

Suddenly he sprang upright.

"A fish!" he yelled. "Another *huge* one!" He jerked his head around and stared at his father. "I thought Amorim said it was halfway to the end of the net!"

"Never mind what Amorim said," his father replied. "Let's get this one now."

He handed the spear to his son. Five minutes later the fish lay in the bottom of the boat. Tiago and his father pushed on toward the end of their net.

"Another one!" Tiago yelled. This time a broad smile lit up his face as he looked back at his father.

Alexandre stepped to the front of the boat and squinted into the water, darker now in the dimming light of the day. Several seconds later he pointed a little ahead of the fish Tiago had spotted.

"Two!" he cried out. "Look!"

Tiago looked. "And in front of them is another one!" he exclaimed.

"Son," said Alexandre joyfully, "we're going to have to do some night fishing." He picked up the short knife and handed it to Tiago. "Dive down and get it. We'll bring them in one at a time."

An hour later Tiago and Alexandre landed their boat with 10 huge fish—six-footers, all of them—and 15 smaller ones!

Amorim stood speechless as they unloaded the fish onto the shore and pushed their boat back out into the water.

"Everyone to their nets!" Tiago heard Amorim yell as he and his father shoved into the water again. Tiago turned and looked. In the dim light of the last bit of dusk, he saw Amorim dash toward his boat about 100 feet down the beach.

All night Tiago and his father felt their way along their net, bringing in the fish. It was nearly noon the next day before their task was done. Amorim and Diaglo walked up as father and son unloaded the last fish from their boat.

"Well, how did your fishing go?" Alexandre asked, a warm smile on his face.

Amorim glanced at Diaglo out of the corner of his

eye, then stared down at the sand. He shrugged his shoulders. "Nothing," he said quietly, and he and Diaglo walked away.

Tiago's mouth dropped open. He looked at his father. "And we caught 122 big ones!" he exclaimed. "And many, many smaller ones!"

Then a smile broke across his face. He motioned toward the mountain of fish on the sand. "It looks as though there will be enough to make a sizable gift to the Lord for building our new church, doesn't it?" Tiago said to his father.

Alexandre laid an arm across Tiago's shoulder. Father and son stood a moment looking at their tremendous catch. "I'd say that you're just about right," Alexandre replied.

22

Misty's Choice

by Denise Jones

Misty pushed open the locker room door and stormed inside to change from her gym clothes into jeans and a sweater before the rest of the team could follow. Their triumphant cheering rang in her ears as the coach continued to explain the announcement that had sent Misty rushing from the gym.

He and the fifth-grade basketball coach at Stanfield had had a rivalry between them for months. Finally the Stanfield coach had agreed on a match. The game would be played the following Saturday.

Two bright splotches of color burned red across Misty's cheeks as she finished dressing and hurried from the auditorium to her next class. Only Amanda, her best friend and fellow teammate, noticed her hasty departure, and she hurried from the locker room to catch up.

"What's the matter with you?" she asked Misty. "Aren't you happy about the Saturday match?"

Misty felt her whole body sag. "Oh, Amanda," she said, "I can't play this Saturday. It's my Sabbath."

Amanda stopped short. "But you've got to play," she said, her voice rising. "You're our best player. That's not a good enough reason to not play."

"To me it is," Misty said firmly. But her heart was in her throat.

As history class progressed, she noticed all the smiling faces eager for Saturday, and she began to ask herself if "the Sabbath" was a good reason. She wanted to play very badly. This game was as important to her as it was to the rest of the team, and Amanda was right—they were depending on her.

Surely God doesn't intend for me to give up something I love so much, she thought. *Surely He wouldn't mind just this once.*

That night after dinner she told her mother about the game, and with a defiant shrug of her shoulders she said, "So I won't be going to church with you and Dad this Sabbath. I've asked Amanda to ask her parents if they can pick me up, so you won't have to wait on me."

"I see," her mother said quietly. She paused. "Before you commit yourself, will you do something for me?"

"What?" Misty asked, a bit suspicious.

"Will you pray very hard about it?"

"OK," Misty answered. But at bedtime she found it hard to pray. She didn't really want to ask God's help. Deep down in her heart she knew what His answer would be. Instead she crawled under the covers without having prayed at all. *I'll pray about it in the morning before I leave for school,* she told herself.

Morning came, and because it was storming and she had to rush to find her raincoat and umbrella, Misty didn't have time to pray. As she hurried through the cold rain to the waiting bus, she told herself it really didn't matter. But she felt a little guilty as she remembered that this Sabbath was her turn to help Mrs. Robinson with the cradle roll class at church.

A frown of aggravation settled on her face as she turned toward the window. Outside, the rain made a soft gray background for the changing autumn colors. Watching the rain through the window reminded her of how badly their little farming community needed rain. Somehow she was reluctantly thankful for the gifts God gives His children.

When Misty opened her lunch box that afternoon in the cafeteria, a little white slip of paper fell on the table. Picking it up, she read in her mother's handwriting, "'If you love me, you will obey what I command'" (John 14:15).

Excusing herself from the table, Misty fled to the empty fifth-grade classroom where nobody could see her tears. She felt miserable. Before now, Sabbaths had always been a blessing. They made her feel happy and close to God. Today she was very unhappy with Sabbaths and herself.

Finally, Misty folded her hands and poured out her heart to God. When at last she said Amen, she felt a lot better and decided to find Mr. Cook, the coach, and tell him she couldn't play in the Saturday morning game.

"Hi, Mr. Cook," she said as she entered his office.

"Misty, I'm glad you're here," he remarked. "The game has been postponed until Sunday afternoon. It seems the coach over there will be out of town Saturday. Will you help me tell the rest of the team?"

During family worship that evening, Misty told her family about the lesson she'd learned that week. "If we ask God, He will help us to do what is right."

As her family bowed their heads, she thanked God for His guiding Spirit. And once again the Sabbath became a blessing for Misty.

23

The Empty Water Jar

by Soledad Caberte as told to Ella Ruth Elkins

When evangelistic meetings were held in the Philippines, Eutiquis and Tessie Gripo, a young farm couple, attended the meetings night after night. Their hearts were touched by what they were hearing, and before long they were baptized and joined the local Adventist church.

One of the many new things Eutiquis and Tessie learned was to reverence the Sabbath. It was very important to them to have their cows, carabao, goats, chickens, and even their harvested corn taken care of before the Sabbath hours.

One Friday afternoon as Tessie was hurrying about, she glanced at their large empty water jar with a tired look. *I don't have time to fill the jar with water now,* she thought, *or I might not be able to finish all my work before sundown.*

So Tessie and Eutiquis hurried doubly fast to put their animals away and to gather in their harvested corn. They were so tired and thirsty. How they wished their water jar at home had been full so that they could have taken some water with them to the fields.

At last all the corn was gathered in. The sun was still shining above the treetops as Tessie and Eutiquis hurried to the house to get ready for the Sabbath. Tessie grabbed a smaller water jug and hurried outdoors to get fresh water to fill the big jar that still stood empty.

As the water began to run into the smaller jar, it got heavier and heavier. When it was half full, it felt so heavy that Tessie was afraid she'd never make it back to the house without dropping it. So she decided not to fill it any more. Oh, how heavy that water seemed to be!

When she finally got home, she started pouring the water from the smaller water jug into the big jar, wondering how many more trips she'd have to make with a heavy load like that before the big jar was filled. Four trips might do it. She groaned inside.

The water from the small jar just kept coming and coming! Tessie's eyes grew wide with astonishment! The big 38-liter jar was now full from the half-filled smaller jug she had just poured in! There was plenty of water for the Sabbath, and she would not have to go back for more!

"Eutiquis!" she called excitedly. "Come look at this water jar! It's full! Did you pour water in there when I wasn't looking?"

"No, I didn't," answered her husband. "But maybe God did when He saw how hard you were working to get everything done before sundown."

And so that is what Tessie believed. Her neighbors frowned when she told them what had happened, but Tessie knew what she had seen. She was greatly encouraged as she thought about her caring and loving God.

24

Keeping the Faith

by Gladys Delong with Glen Robinson

It was a rainy day in 1917, and my brother, Jim, was bored and looking for something to do.

"Why don't you read a book from the bookcase?" Mom suggested from the other room.

"Mom, I've read every book we own more than once," Jim said, sighing. "I can't bear to read any of them again!" He looked out in frustration at the pouring rain.

"How about this one?" 9-year-old Ivan, our little brother, asked, holding up a book. "I found it behind the bookshelf."

Jim took it and looked at the cover. *"Bible Footlights.* Sounds like a religious book for old folks. Well, at least I haven't read it before."

Jim and Ivan went back to the bedroom they shared. Ivan lay on the floor with paper and pencil, and Jim threw himself across his bed and flipped through the pages of the book.

"That must be some book you found there," his dad said when Jim brought the book to the dinner table with him.

"Yes," Jim responded, his eyes still focused on the page he was reading.

"Well, interesting or not, you need to put it away until after dinner," Dad said. Jim nodded and closed the book, putting it on the floor beside his chair. Jim, Ivan, and the rest of the family bowed their heads, and Dad asked God's blessing on the food.

"So what does the book say that's so interesting?" Mom asked Jim as she passed him some green beans.

"Lots of things," he responded. "And all the claims it makes are based on the Bible."

"Oh, really," Dad responded quietly.

"Yes, it includes Bible verses that prove what it says." Jim chewed on a mouthful of food before continuing. "But there was one chapter that really surprised me. It says that the Sabbath is really Saturday and not Sunday. God made Sabbath on the seventh day of the week—that's Saturday—and people tried to change it to the first day of the week, Sunday."

Jim's words met with stony silence. Everyone in the family continued to eat, but no one dared speak, waiting for Dad to respond. Finally Jim couldn't stand the silence anymore.

"Dad, did you and Mom know that? I mean, why do we and all the other families go to church on Sunday if Saturday is the true Sabbath?"

Mom looked over at Dad in silence. He wiped his mouth before he responded.

"Jim, there are a lot of reasons we go to church on Sunday. Your mother and I have always gone to church on Sunday, and everyone we know goes to church on Sunday. It wouldn't be right for us to change just because of what a book says."

Jim looked at his father in surprise. "But Dad, if God made Saturday as the Sabbath, then it would be wrong to continue to worship on the wrong day, wouldn't it?"

"Wrong or not, Sunday is our Sabbath," Dad responded. "That's the way I was raised, and that's the way we've raised you. We're not going to change that just because of what someone wrote in a book!"

Jim shook his head as he and Ivan headed for their room after dinner. "The book uses so many Bible verses to prove that the seventh day is the Sabbath," he said. "It can't be wrong, and yet Mom and Dad don't see the mistake they're making."

Ivan shrugged. "Maybe you misunderstood. Maybe you need to go back and read it some more."

Jim thought about it and nodded. "Maybe you're right. I'll go back and read it again, and maybe I'll understand it better."

Jim continued to study the book and compare it to his Bible. For several days he also thought and thought about what he had read.

"Do you have it figured out?" Ivan asked him one day.

"I've studied and studied, and decided that the book is right. Saturday, not Sunday, is the Sabbath. And if Sunday is not the Sabbath, I don't want to worship on that day anymore!"

"But what about Dad?" Ivan asked. "Won't he be angry?"

"He'll be mad, all right," Jim said. "As for what to do, I don't know yet."

The whole issue of Saturday or Sunday weighed heavily on Jim's mind. He loved his father and didn't want to disobey him, but his parents had also taught him to do what was right, regardless of the consequences.

That night Jim knelt by his bed and prayed. "Dear God, I'm confused about what to do. Please show me in a dream tonight if Saturday is the true Sabbath. If it is, dear God, I promise You I will keep it holy for the rest of my life!" Feeling better about the situation, Jim climbed into bed and went to sleep.

The next thing Jim knew, he felt a hand on his shoulder shaking him awake. He looked up into the face of what he realized was an angel! The heavenly messenger smiled, but Jim realized that the angel had an important reason for his visit.

"Get up, Jim, and go to the window," the angel said. "Look out at the sky. If the sky is a bright glowing red, you will know that Saturday is the true Sabbath."

Jim got out of bed and went to the window. He raised the shade and looked out. Everywhere he looked, the sky glowed bright red. He knew that his prayer had been answered.

"Dear God," he prayed, "thank You for answering my prayer. I promise You that from now on for the rest of my life I will keep the seventh-day Sabbath holy." He did not know that this decision would make his life very difficult in the weeks to come.

On Saturday morning Dad was ready to go to work. He called the boys together to assign their chores for the day.

"Jim, today I want you to go to the cornfield and hoe the corn. Make sure you get all the weeds out," he said to my older brother.

"But, Dad," Jim said, "today is the Sabbath. I can't work today."

Dad laughed. "You must have your days mixed up, Jim. Today is Saturday, not Sunday. *Tomorrow* is the Sabbath."

"No, Dad," Jim replied. "*Today* is God's Sabbath, and I can't work on the day He's made holy."

Dad's usually kind and loving expression turned hard and serious. "Now, you listen to me," Dad said to Jim in a tone that scared him. "Enough of this nonsense about Saturday being the Sabbath. You just want to have two days to rest. I promise you this, if that cornfield isn't hoed and weeded when I get home tonight, I'll give you a whipping you won't forget." With that, Dad left for his job on the railroad.

"Do you think he meant it, Jim?" Ivan asked as the boys headed back toward the house. "Will Dad really give you a whipping if you don't work today?"

"You know Dad as well as I do," Jim responded. "He always means what he says."

"Then what are you going to do?" Ivan asked, struggling to keep up with him.

Jim didn't respond. Instead he walked into the kitchen where Mom was wiping off the kitchen table.

"Mom, will you fix me a lunch?" Jim asked. "I'm going into the woods today. I'm going to keep the Sabbath holy."

Mom sighed. "All right, Jim. I'll fix you a lunch."

A few minutes later Jim headed off to the woods to keep his Sabbath appointment with God. Crossing the pasture, he suddenly heard a noise behind him. He turned and saw Ivan struggling to catch up with him.

"Ivan, what are you doing here?" he asked in surprise.

"I'm going to the woods to keep the Sabbath holy," Ivan said. "Just like you."

"But you know that Dad will whip you too," Jim pointed out.

"I know," he said, shrugging his skinny shoulders. "But I'm still going into the woods with you to keep the Sabbath holy."

Jim let Ivan follow him into the woods, where they stayed all day. They read the Bible and the new book that Jim had discovered, and they prayed together. Finally the sun began to set, and the boys walked home slowly, knowing what was waiting for them there.

Dad stood in the front yard with a big switch in his hand. First, he whipped Jim hard. Then he whipped Ivan as well.

"Next Saturday," he told the boys as they wiped the tears from their eyes, "maybe you'll do as you are told."

Saturday came around again, and Dad again gathered the boys to assign their chores. Once again Jim told his dad, "This is the Sabbath. I can't work today."

Dad's face grew red with anger. "If the work I gave you today isn't done when I get home tonight," he said, "I'll beat you worse than I beat you last Saturday night."

Dad left for work. Once again Jim asked Mom for a lunch so he could go to the woods and keep the Sabbath holy. And once again Ivan followed him into the woods to keep the Sabbath with him.

That evening Dad was in the yard again, waiting for the boys to come home. The longer he waited, the angrier he became. Just before dark the boys walked into the yard. Dad grabbed Jim and started beating him with a switch. He whipped him and whipped him until Mom ran out of the house and pleaded, "Stop! You've whipped him enough!"

All during the week Jim prayed, "Dear God, I can't stand another beating like Dad gave me last Saturday night. Please, dear God, when Dad gives me work to do next Sabbath, please let something happen so I can't do it. Let it not be my fault so Dad can't whip me again."

When Saturday came, Dad said, "Jim, I have a job for you. Yesterday I bought some chickens from a man who is moving away. I want you to take this buggy and go get those chickens. If those chickens aren't in the chicken coop when I get home tonight, I'll beat you worse than ever!"

Jim was worried. Would it be breaking the Sabbath to go get the chickens? "Lord," he prayed, "please do something to keep me from going. And make it not my fault so Dad won't whip me tonight."

This time Jim wouldn't let Ivan follow him, especially since Dad had not given Ivan permission. Jim called Old Ned, the horse, from the pasture and hitched him to the buggy. When he had attached the thick leather harness, Jim drove Old Ned out of the yard and down the steep hill from their house.

Suddenly he heard a loud *pop,* and the horse stopped.

That sounded like a gunshot! Jim thought, but he saw that Old Ned was not hurt. Jim got out of the buggy and went to see what the problem was. When he saw it, he knew that God had answered his prayer.

Jim unhitched Old Ned and put him back in the pasture. Then he called Mom out to the barn to show her what had happened. He told her what he had prayed, and she said, "God has answered your prayer, son. Go in the house, and I'll fix you a lunch so you can go to the woods and keep your Sabbath holy."

That night Dad came home from work and immediately saw that the new chickens were not in the chicken coop. He stormed into the kitchen, where Mom was preparing supper.

"Where is that boy?" he shouted. "I'll beat him within an inch of his life!"

"Before you do *anything*," Mom said to Dad, "take a look at the horse's harness." Then she told him about Jim's prayer and what had happened on his way to pick up the chickens.

Dad went out to the barn and checked the harness. He discovered that the front strap of the harness, made of leather so thick that no human being could pull it apart, had been torn in half! Jim *couldn't* fetch the chickens, because the horse could no longer pull the buggy.

Dad returned to the house, his face as white as a sheet. "That boy didn't cut that strap," he said to

Mom. "No human hand could have torn that strap in two! When Jim gets home, I'll tell him that from now on he can keep his Sabbath holy."

And that's how Jim, my older brother, through his faithfulness, lived to see his nine brothers and sisters, his mother and father, many family members, and many of his friends become Sabbathkeeping Christians. Today, many years later, people are still learning of the Sabbath because of what a 14-year-old boy did so long ago.